150
FAMOUS
SCOTS

LILY SEAFIELD

WAVERLEY BOOKS

This edition published 2009 by Waverley Books, David Dale House,
New Lanark, ML11 9DJ

Text by Lily Seafield and RLS

Copyright © Waverley Books 2009

ISBN 978-1-902407-14-2

Printed and bound in the UK

ADAM, ROBERT
(1728–1792)
Architect

Robert Adam was born in Kirkcaldy in Fife. He was the second-oldest son of architect William Adam. He was educated in Edinburgh and in the mid 1740s he joined his father's firm. From 1754 to 1758 he travelled in Europe to continue his studies and spent a great deal of time in Italy, where he studied buildings, both classical and contemporary. When he returned to Great Britain from Italy, he set up a practice in London where he was joined by his younger brother James, who became junior partner in the firm. Robert was appointed Architect of the King's Works in 1761, an honoured position which he held until 1769 when he was succeeded by James, and he and his brother enjoyed considerable success as the most fashionable architects in the capital city.

The style of ornamentation in the building works in which they were involved drew much inspiration from a variety of classical models. The interiors created by Robert Adam were particularly distinctive, with ornate plasterwork adding grace to walls and ceilings. The painstaking attention to detail in an Adam designed interior was very impressive.

Adam's work was greatly in demand, particularly in the country houses of England's wealthy nobility. Work poured in and Adam's fame and influence grew throughout Europe, but in the late 1760s, he and his brother were brought to the brink of ruin after embarking upon the Adelphi project, involving the design and construction of a terrace of houses by the Thames in London. It was a particularly ambitious undertaking that overstretched their resources and was a catastrophe in financial terms, with the twenty-four houses in the terrace ultimately having to be disposed of by lottery. Adam returned to Scotland in 1782 and lived and worked there for the rest of his life.

Some of the finest examples of his work in Scotland are Culzean Castle in Ayrshire, the Old Quad of Edinburgh University, Register House in Edinburgh and Charlotte Square, also in Edinburgh.

ARROL, WILLIAM
(1839–1913)
ENGINEER

William Arrol was born in Houston in Renfrewshire. His family was far from wealthy and in order to supplement the family income, young William had to find work in a thread factory when he was barely ten years of age. When he reached the age of fourteen he secured a position as an apprentice blacksmith and engineer. He was extremely dedicated to this new career and followed up his practical learning experience with studies at night school, where he learnt the principles and theories of mechanics and engineering. His efforts paid off and he was able eventually to set himself up in his own engineering business in 1868.

His hard work and enterprise were remarkable and this was a considerable achievement for a man as young as he was, from such humble origins. He undertook a variety of planning and building works, but he was destined to work mainly on the construction of bridges during his career.

Two of his most famous projects were the new bridge over the River Tay and the Forth Railway Bridge, both of which stand as monuments to his skill today. The former was begun in 1882, three years after the disastrous collapse of the first bridge, and it was completed and opened in 1887. The latter was begun in 1883 and completed in 1890. Arrol's next major project took him to London, where he was responsible for the construction of Tower Bridge. This project took eight years to complete, from 1886 to 1894. William Arrol was knighted in 1890 in recognition of his great work and served as a Member of Parliament from 1892 to 1906. He died in 1913, aged 74.

ATHOLL, KATHARINE MARJORY, DUCHESS OF
(1864–1960)
POLITICIAN AND ANTI-FASCIST CAMPAIGNER

Katharine, Duchess of Atholl was born Katharine Ramsay and was the daughter of Sir James Ramsay of Bamff, near Alyth in Perthshire. She attended Wimbledon High School and showing promise as a gifted pianist, she progressed to the Royal College of Music, hoping to follow a musical career. Her life changed direction when, in July 1899, she became married to the Marquis of Tullibardine, the future

8th Duke of Atholl. They went to live at Blair Castle in Perthshire and in 1917 she became the Duchess of Atholl. She edited *The Military History of Perthshire*, published in 1908. During the war, she played an active part in the organisation of concerts and entertainments for the troops overseas. She took an active interest in her husband's political career in the early years of their marriage, before he succeeded to the dukedom, and this led to her own involvement in politics in later years.

In 1923 she campaigned successfully as Conservative candidate for Kinross and Perthshire, becoming the first Scottish woman Member of Parliament. She followed this 'first' with another when she became the first Conservative woman cabinet minister in 1924. She served in the cabinet as a minister at the Department of Education until 1929. Whilst working in this post she became a dedicated champion of the underprivileged, and worked hard to ensure that the educational needs of poorer children were not overlooked in matters of policy. Her interest in child welfare was not confined to her own country and she campaigned vigorously for fairer treatment of both women and children in the countries of the British Empire.

In the 1930s she became deeply concerned by the rise of fascism in Spain and in Germany, and published her own translation of *Mein Kampf* in an effort to give warning of the dangers of Hitler's rise to power. Increasingly, as she became more outspoken against fascism, she found herself in conflict with the Conservative government over their policies and she resigned her seat in parliament in 1938 after a dispute over the Munich Agreement. She lost the by-election which followed, but the outbreak of the Second World War proved her fears of the threat which Hitler posed to Europe to have been well-founded. The Duke of Atholl died in 1942, but Katharine remained active in campaigns at home and abroad until her death in 1960.

BAIRD, JOHN LOGIE
(1888–1946)
ELECTRICAL ENGINEER, INVENTOR OF TELEVISION

John Logie Baird was born in Helensburgh. When he left school (Glasgow Academy) he continued his education at Glasgow Royal Technical College, where he studied electrical engineering. His future looked unpromising for a while. He spent a brief period working for the Clyde Valley Electricity company but resigned on grounds of ill-health. He went to live in the West Indies for a short period before returning to England and eventually settling in Hastings.

He worked on various ideas for inventions and innovations but became particularly interested in the possibilities of television transmission. In 1926, he succeeded in constructing a crude form of television transmitter and receiver, capable of sending mechanically scanned pictures from one room to the next. As his work progressed he managed to demonstrate the ability to send television pictures countrywide and then across the Atlantic. The first television pictures that he produced consisted of thirty lines and were of very poor quality, but by 1936 he was able to produce two-hundred-and-forty-line images. In spite of this considerable progress, the BBC, who had been using the Baird system since 1929, opted in 1937 to replace it with a more sophisticated system, consisting of more than four hundred lines, electronically rather than mechanically scanned. This system had been invented by Marconi, the Italian physicist. Undaunted by this setback to his fortunes, and without the benefit of any form of public or private financial backing for the work which he was pursuing, Baird continued to follow his interest in television, and was able eventually to produce pictures in colour. His other work included valuable research into radar and the invention of a night vision (infrared) camera. He was still working when he died, aged 58, in 1946.

BARRIE, SIR JAMES MATTHEW (JM)
(1860–1937)
Novelist and playwright

James Matthew Barrie was born in Kirriemuir, Angus. His father was a weaver. James spent his schooldays at Forfar Academy and Dumfries Academy and then progressed to Edinburgh University. After his graduation in 1882 he worked for a short time as a journalist in Nottingham. He moved to London in 1885 and made regular contributions to the *St James's Gazette* and the *British Weekly*. He had limited success with his early novels, but when *A Window in Thrums*, a series of sketches of Scottish life inspired by his home town of Kirriemuir, was published in 1889, it was received more favourably and the work which followed, *The Little Minister*, was a success. Barrie was to dramatise the latter work in later years.

Barrie began to focus his work on writing for the stage in the 1890s, although he published three further novels, *Margaret Ogilvy* in 1896 and *Sentimental Tommy* and *Tommy and Grizel* in 1895 and 1900 respectively. His plays were a success, both in Britain and in America, and they included *Walker, London* (1893), *The Professor's Love Story* (1894), *Quality Street* (1902) and *The Admirable Crichton* (1902). His most memorable and appealing work is universally recognised as *Peter Pan, or The Boy Who Wouldn't Grow Up*, which was premiered on the stage in 1904. It remains a favourite with adults and children to this day. Barrie's later works such as *Dear Brutus* (1917) and *Mary Rose* (1920) demonstrated a continuing interest in fantasy and fairies.

Barrie was married in 1894 to Mary Ansell, but the marriage was a failure and ended in an acrimonious divorce in 1909.

Barrie was honoured with various awards during his life and was awarded honorary degrees in several universities, including St Andrews, Oxford and Edinburgh. He was made a baronet in 1913 and in 1930 was appointed as Chancellor of the University of Edinburgh. He died in June, 1937 and was buried in his birthplace of Kirriemuir.

BARRY, MIRANDA 'JAMES'
(*c.*1790–1865)
Surgeon

During her life as a doctor, Doctor 'James' Barry achieved high status and earned the respect of her peers in the medical profession and in the British Army. However, she did so not as a woman, but as a man.

After her death she earned even greater fame when it was revealed that she had kept her astounding secret, from all those who knew her and worked with her, for over fifty years.

'James' Barry's real name was Miranda Barry, and so dedicated was she to following the profession of her choosing, in what was at that time a male-only world, that she was prepared to maintain her masquerade from the time of her application to study medicine at Edinburgh University until her death in 1865.

'James' graduated as a doctor in 1812 and instead of opting for a quieter life in private practice, applied to join the Army Medical Service in 1813. She took up her first post as a surgeon's assistant and rose through the ranks, until in 1857 she was posted to Canada, promoted to Inspector-General of military hospitals in Quebec and Montreal. Her work as a military doctor took her all over the world, including the Caribbean, Africa, the East Indies and the Mediterranean. She took a particular interest in preventative medicine, concerning herself with improving the welfare of the soldiers and the conditions under which they lived. Barry was reputed to have had a fine intellect but also a fearsome temper, and was involved in several duels. However, it was also said of her that 'No man could show such sympathy for one in pain', and she is said to have carried out the first caesarian section in the English-speaking world when posted to South Africa. She could be entertaining and flamboyant company. She died in retirement in England in 1865, when finally, posthumously, her secret was revealed. She is buried in Kendal Rise cemetery, London.

BAXTER, STANLEY
(1926–)
ACTOR, COMEDIAN

A Glaswegian, born into a middle-class family, Stanley's career in show business was encouraged by his mother and discouraged by his father. His astonishing gift for mimicry was already strong at the age of seven. At Hillhead High School he wrote and produced a revue, and was spotted by Kathleen Garscadden, the formidable head of the BBC's children's programmes in Scotland, who employed him to read serial adventure stories. He studied at the Royal Scottish Academy of Music, but returned to comedy as a national serviceman, drafted into the Entertainment Unit, then joined the Glasgow Citizens Theatre and participated in its years of renown. On radio, he became a familiar voice and, following a move to London, the TV comedy series *On the Bright Side* widened his audience. A lifelong student of Glaswegian speech, *Parliamo Glasgow* linked his pleasure in words with his genius for – usually gentle

– satire. In 1963 he had his first TV show, *The Stanley Baxter Show*, but he also relished live performance in the pantomime season. Most memorable, perhaps, were his TV spectaculars of the 1980s, whose extravagant costuming, props and scenery burst programme budgets, and made some critics wonder whether Baxter's comic genius really needed such lavish back-up. Baxter's wife Moira died in 1997, after 46 years of marriage. They had no children. He was honoured by his profession with a Lifetime Achievement award at the 1997 British Comedy Awards.

BELL, ALEXANDER GRAHAM
(1847–1922)
TEACHER OF THE DEAF, INVENTOR OF THE TELEPHONE

Alexander Graham Bell was born in Edinburgh. He was the son of Alexander Melville Bell, founder of the science of phonetics. He was educated in Edinburgh and in London and he joined his father in his work, studying the mechanics of speech and teaching the deaf. In 1870, he emigrated to Canada and a year later moved to America. There, in Boston, he continued the work he had begun with his father, helping deaf children to communicate through speech. He founded a school that became absorbed by the University of Boston and he was appointed Professor of Vocal Physiology.

In his spare time, Bell was preoccupied with experimenting with the idea of transmitting speech. Without the benefit of any formal training in electronic science, he continued doggedly with his experiments, basing his work on the theory that it should be possible to transmit sound along telegraph wires. In 1875, he met with success. His assistant, listening in a neighbouring room, heard his first transmitted words; 'Watson, come here; I want you,' spoken over a crude apparatus which little resembled the telephone we use today, but that was its direct ancestor. His design was patented in 1876 and the Bell Telephone Company was formed the following year. He was awarded the Volta Prize by the French government in 1880 and with the money he was given, he founded the Volta Laboratory in Washington. Continuing his work there, he invented the photophone in 1880 and the graphophone in 1887. Bell was also responsible for the invention of the audiometer. His interests in a wide variety of scientific matters led to him founding the journal *Science* in 1883 and in his later years, he carried out several experiments in the field of aeronautics.

Although his success with his inventions made him an immensely wealthy man, Bell never lost his interest in studying the nature and causes of deafness and in teaching deaf children to speak. He was a generous contributor to related charities.

Bell died in Nova Scotia in August, 1922.

BELLANY, JOHN
(1942–)
Painter

Born in Port Seton, East Lothian, Bellany is most famous for his depictions of coastal scenes and harbours. The

East Coast fishing community also features prominently in his work. He studied painting at Edinburgh School of Art from 1960–65, and the Royal College of Art in London from 1965–68. His first solo exhibition was in Holland in 1965, and since then he has had exhibitions in many galleries, in the USA, Australia and Europe as well as in Great Britain. From 1968 to 1984 he taught art in Brighton, Winchester and London. In more recent years he has suffered from ill health, which itself has been taken as a theme for his paintings. In 2005 he suffered two heart attacks. He has received many awards and honorary doctorates, and was made CBE in 1994.

BENSON, HARRY JAMES
(1929–)
PHOTOGRAPHER

'A lone lensman from Scotland with a hungry eye' was how one commentator summed up this celebrated photographer. Born in Glasgow, where his father was a curator at Calder Park Zoo, he began as a wedding photographer, specialising in high-speed development. His pictures appeared in Glasgow papers and in 1956 he moved to London, to work first for the *Daily Sketch*, then the *Daily Express*. Benson's skills as a press photographer have become legendary. The breakthrough came in 1964 when he travelled with the Beatles to the USA (his first visit there) taking the celebrated shot of their pillow fight when 'I Want to Hold Your Hand' reached Number One. His range of portraits covers US presidents and film stars. But what has always distinguished Benson's work is that there is something of the paparazzo in him: the ability to be in the right place at the right time and get the definitive shot. Benson, who lives in New York, was awarded a CBE in the New Year Honours of 2009.

BLAIR, TONY (ANTHONY CHARLES LYNTON)
(1953–)
Middle East Envoy and Former Prime Minister of Great Britain

Tony Blair was born in Edinburgh. He was educated in Durham, then in Edinburgh where he attended the exclusive Fettes College in the city. He progressed to Oxford University and after graduation studied for the Bar. His speciality was trade union and industrial law. In 1983, he entered the House of Commons as MP for the constituency of Sedgefield. He rose rapidly through the ranks and in 1984 became Opposition Spokesman on Treasury and Economic Affairs, remaining in this post until 1987. He then served in the Department of Trade and Industry for one year, the Department of Energy for one year and The Department of Employment for three years. In 1992, he became Opposition Home Affairs Spokesman. After the death of John Smith in 1994, Blair became Leader of the Labour party and under his leadership, Labour underwent a series of reforms, including the updating of Clause IV of the party constitution. The Labour draft manifesto based on pledges concerning education, employment, crime, health and economic stability, faced very little opposition amongst party members when it was put to the vote in 1996. New Labour under Tony Blair was voted into power in a landslide victory in 1997. Blair is the youngest man to have become Leader of the Labour Party and the third youngest Prime Minister in history.

Two of the most notable accomplishments of Blair's New Labour were achieved within one year of his coming to power. Referendums took place in Scotland and Wales, in which voters elected for a Scottish parliament and a Welsh assembly with devolved powers. The peace talks in Northern Ireland moved forward with renewed vigour and in 1998, a peace plan was formulated and approved by referendum. Britain's involvement in the Iraq war of 2003 was a major cause of public discontent, the consequences of which plagued Blair for the remainder of his premiership. Accusations that he misled parliament in order to lead Britain into the war caused his popularity to decrease and this showed in the 2005 general election, which Labour still won, but without the landslide victory of the previous two elections. He stood down as Prime Minister in 2007, to be succeeded by Gordon Brown. He is now Middle East Envoy on behalf of the United Nations, the European Union, the United States and Russia.

Blair is married to Cherie Booth, a prominent lawyer and judge. They have four children, the youngest of whom, Leo, was born in May, 2000. He is the Labour

Party's longest-serving Prime Minister and the only Labour leader to have had three consecutive general election victories.

BOSWELL, JAMES
(1740–1795)
WRITER

James Boswell was born in Edinburgh. His father was Lord Auchinleck, a judge. Boswell studied law at the universities of Edinburgh and Glasgow but had no real interest in the legal profession, preferring instead to cultivate interesting and powerful social contacts. He ran away to London in 1760 and there, in a state of religious crisis, was converted to Roman Catholicism. He remained in London, living the high life and dreaming of joining the army, until he was persuaded to return to Glasgow to continue his law studies. In 1762 after his graduation, he returned to London where, on the 16th May, 1763, he first met Dr Samuel Johnson and they became intimate friends. Boswell left London the following year, ostensibly to continue his legal studies in Utrecht, but he stayed there only briefly and moved on to Germany, where he managed to engineer meetings with both Voltaire and Rousseau. From Germany he travelled to Corsica, where he made the acquaintance of hero and patriot Pasquale Paoli. This encounter led to the publication of Boswell's *Account of Corsica* (1768) which was very successful.

After a series of love affairs, Boswell returned to Edinburgh and finally submitted to marriage in 1769.

His wife was his cousin, Margaret Montgomery. He did not stay long in Edinburgh and by 1773 he was back in London, enjoying the company of intellectuals and aristocrats and was now a member of the Literary Club. His friendship with Samuel Johnson remained strong and in 1773 the two of them embarked upon a tour of the Hebrides, which was chronicled by Johnson in *Journey to the Western Isles of Scotland* and by Boswell in *Journal of a Tour to the Hebrides*. In the course of this tour, they met with Flora Macdonald.

Boswell returned to Edinburgh, but continued to make trips to London to visit Johnson. In the late 1770s he contributed a number of articles to the *London Magazine* under the pseudonym of 'The Hypochodriack'. In 1782, his father died and two years later, Johnson also passed away. Boswell set to work on a biography of Johnson, but did not complete it for publication until 1791. *Journal of a Tour of the Hebrides* was published in 1785. His wife died in 1789, and Boswell, already a heavy drinker, turned increasingly to alcohol for solace and inspiration. He died in London in May 1795.

Boswell's literary abilities were not fully recognised until his private papers were discovered in Ireland and in Scotland between 1926 and 1930. His journals, published in the 1950s, established his reputation posthumously, as a writer and journalist of considerable talent.

BROWN, JAMES GORDON
(1951–)
Politician, Prime Minster of Great Britain

The future premier was born in Govan, Glasgow, but his father became parish minister of Kirkcaldy when Brown was three, and Fife has always been his home and base. As part of a 'fast-track' educational experiment, he went to Kirkcaldy High School when only ten, sat his leaving exams two years early and went to Edinburgh University at 16. He was to criticise his 'e-stream' education as 'materially and mentally harmful'. In his first week of university he suffered a detached retina in his right eye, thought to be as the result of a rugby kick. He lost sight in this eye and has only partial vision in the other. This appears to have stiffened an already determined nature. Graduating with a First at 20, he immediately stood for the office of University Rector and won, in a highly-organised campaign, turning the honorific position into an effective chairmanship. He was also moving into Labour politics and by the time he was elected as MP for Dunfermline East in 1983, he was a seasoned political infighter ready to take his skills to Westminster. His historic partnership with Tony Blair in the formation of 'New Labour' was swiftly formed. But in 1994 it was Blair who emerged as party leader. After the Labour victory of 1997 Brown began a ten-year run as Chancellor, during which he regularly claimed to have ended 'boom and bust' politics. When Blair resigned, Brown became party leader by acclamation, and thus also Prime Minister.

In his premiership's first four months he did well in the polls despite facing some serious challenges – including terrorist attempts on London and Glasgow and sever flooding in parts on England. However his approach seemed increasingly uncertain, even inept at times. As the signs of economic recession grew more obvious in 2008–09, Brown was compelled to overturn every economic policy of the previous decade in the effort to prevent a recession from turning into a prolonged slump. In 2000 Brown married Sarah Macauley. They have two sons.

BROWN, JOHN
(1826–1883)
SERVANT OF QUEEN VICTORIA

John Brown was born at Craithenaird, Balmoral, in Aberdeenshire. His father was a crofter. Brown was employed as ghillie to Prince Albert on the Royal estate at Balmoral and eventually became the personal attendant of Queen Victoria. After the death of Prince Albert in 1861, the Queen grieved terribly.

Brown's concern for the Queen and his loyal devotion were instrumental in her recovery from the deep depression that took hold of her after Prince Albert died. With a forthright manner that verged on the rude, he nonetheless had enormous respect for his royal mistress and was fiercely protective of her. His respect was returned by the Queen in equal measure and his relationship with her developed into one of genuine friendship, which was misconstrued in some circles.

The Queen referred to him as her 'Beloved Friend' in the dedication of her *Highland Journal*.

In 1997, the film *Mrs Brown* was released, based on the story of John Brown and Queen Victoria and starring Billy Connolly and Judi Dench.

Some have claimed that Brown and the Queen were secretly married. These rumours resurfaced in 2003 with the publishing of the diaries of Lewis Harcourt, son of Sir William Harcourt who was home secretary of William Gladstone's government. It is said that the Queen's chaplain, Norman Macleod, made a confession on his deathbed that he had married the couple. There has, however, been no proof.

BRUCE, ROBERT
(1274–1329)
King of Scotland

Born in Essex, Robert the Bruce reigned as King of Scotland from 1306. As Earl of Carrick, he swore fealty to Edward I. In 1297, however, he took the part of the Scots in the fight for independence led by William Wallace and in 1298, he was made one of the four regents of the kingdom. In 1302, he returned his allegiance to Edward, but in time came to learn that the king intended to put him to death. He fled to Scotland and stabbed John Comyn, a rival for the Scottish throne, to death at Dumfries. He then made his claim to the throne of Scotland and was crowned at Scone in 1306. His tactics against the English were those of a master of guerrilla warfare. His initial encounters with the English, at Perth and Dalry resulted in defeat. He retired to Rathlin Island and was thought by some to be dead. The popular legend about Robert the Bruce taking heart after watching the valiant efforts of a spider to build a web relate to this period in his life. In 1307 he re-emerged with renewed vigour and defeated the English in battle at Loudon Hill. He continued his campaign to regain Scotland from the English for the next seven years, working his way through the north of Scotland and gathering support. In 1309, while the struggle was still far from over, he held his first parliament at St Andrews. By 1314 he had amassed considerable support and had control of virtually all lands north of the Forth. The Lothian area soon also fell under his control and his legendary success against the forces of Edward II at the Battle of Bannockburn in 1314 marked the end of the civil war in Scotland, but Bruce's struggles against the English continued unabated. He took Berwick in 1318 and fought against English forces in Northumberland and Yorkshire. The English remained aggressive towards Robert the Bruce and in 1320 a congress of 31 Scottish nobles gathered to produce the Declaration of Arbroath, seeking Papal recognition of Scotland as an independent sovereignty with Robert the Bruce as ruler. Recognition was finally granted in 1323. In spite of a treaty with the English, made after the defeat of Edward near Byland Abbey in 1323, hostilities did not cease completely until 1328 when, with Edward III now on the throne, the Treaty of Northampton was drawn up underwriting

English acknowledgement of Robert as sovereign of an independent Scotland. He died the following year and his heart was buried at Melrose Abbey.

Robert the Bruce was married twice. His first wife was Isabella, daughter of the Earl of Mar. She bore him a daughter, Marjory, who was the mother of Robert II. His second wife was Elizabeth, daughter of the earl of Ulster. Their son, David, succeeded his father to the throne of Scotland.

BUCHAN, JOHN 1ST BARON TWEEDSMUIR
(1875–1940)
NOVELIST, BIOGRAPHER

John Buchan, the son of a minister in the Free Church, was born in Perth. He attended Hutcheson's Grammar School in Glasgow and continued his studies at Glasgow University and Brasenose College, Oxford. He graduated with first class honours and was awarded the Newdigate prize for poetry in 1898. Buchan was already a prolific writer in his university years and *Scholar Gypsies*, a collection of essays written by him, was published in 1896. Other early works written by Buchan include *John Burnet of Barns* (1898) and *A Lost Lady of the Old Years* (1899). In 1901, he was called to the Bar and was then appointed to the staff of Lord Milner, the High Commissioner to South Africa, as private secretary. He returned to Scotland in 1903 and continued writing while working as a barrister. He was also appointed as a director of the publishing firm

Nelson's at this time. In 1910, another novel, *Prester John* was published and five years after that, the novel for which he is best known, *The Thirty-Nine Steps*. The main character in this fast-paced spy adventure also appeared in later books, including *Greenmantle* (1916), *Mr Standfast* (1919), and *The Three Hostages* (1924).

During World War I, Buchan worked for the British Government and in 1917, was appointed Director of Information. In 1927 he was elected as MP representing the Scottish universities, a position that he held until 1935, and he was appointed as Lord High Commissioner to the General Assembly of the Church of Scotland in 1933. In 1935, he became Governor-General of Canada. During all this time he continued to write prodigiously, both fiction and non-fiction. In 1937, he was made a privy councillor and was elected Chancellor of Edinburgh University. By the time of his death in 1940, he had received many honours for both his political and literary work and had produced more than 37 works of fiction and more than 100 non-fictional publications, including biographies of JAMES GRAHAM, Marquis of Montrose (1928) and SIR WALTER SCOTT (1932).

BURNS, ROBERT
(1759–1796)
POET

This charismatic figure is surely one of the best known and best loved Scots. Robert Burns was born in Alloway, Ayrshire, the eldest son of a poor tenant farmer, William Burns and his wife, Agnes Broun. In spite of the family's poverty, Robert was given a good literary education and was encouraged by both his parents to read widely and to study the literary and musical traditions of his own people. He was already writing poetry when his father died, leaving him in charge of the family. He rented Mossgiel farm, near Mauchline with his brother Gilbert, but the venture failed. This, combined with a disastrous love affair with Jean Armour, sank the young poet into despair, but his misery was to prove the catalyst behind a prolific spell of writing. The work which resulted was gathered into a volume and published as *Poems, Chiefly in the Scottish Dialect* in Kilmarnock in 1786. Robert had been intending to emigrate but the success of the publication changed his plans.

He travelled to Edinburgh where he was greeted with great enthusiasm by literary society. Another expanded edition of his poems was published in 1787 and he used the proceeds to travel to the Borders and the Highlands. He resumed his relationship with Jean Armour and after a brief flirtation with 'Clarinda' (Agnes [Nancy] Maclehose, with whom he exchanged many romantic letters and poems, but, it is said, for once, he did not have a full-blown affair), he finally married Jean in 1788. He moved with his new wife to Ellisland in Dumfriesshire, where he leased another farm and took up a job as an exciseman. He continued to write ('Tam o' Shanter' dates from this time) and eventually gave up the farm, settling in Dumfries combining excise work with writing in his spare time. Poor health had dogged the poet since early in his life, however, and in 1796 his condition deteriorated steadily and he died from heart disease brought on by rheumatic fever.

The poems and songs of Burns remain popular to this day. His work shows an acute insight into human behaviour, often reflecting his own fiery political views and demonstrating a great talent for caricature and satire. It also shows irony and wit, unashamed romanticism and sentiment, bawdy humour, a seemingly indiscriminate admiration for the fairer sex and a capacity for compassion and feeling for his fellow man. He left behind him a body of work that remains undiminished in importance. Some of the most well-known work includes the following: 'The Cotter's Saturday Night', 'Holy Willie's Prayer', 'Tam o' Shanter', 'The Address to a Mouse' and 'The Address to a Haggis'.

BURRELL, SIR WILLIAM
(1861–1958)
Ship-owner and Benefactor

The son of a ship-owner, third of nine children, Burrell entered the family business at the age of 15, at a time when Glasgow could claim to be the world's shipping metropolis. He became very rich and was able to indulge his passion for art on a royal scale. In 1901 he was one of the backers of the Glasgow International Art Exhibition. His collection of paintings, tapestries, sculptures, rugs, furniture and ceramics eventually numbered over 8000 items. He was knighted in 1927 for his work for the public benefit and for art. In 1944 he presented the collection to the city of Glasgow, with financial provision for a special gallery which would keep the works in prime condition (at that time, air quality in Glasgow was notoriously bad). The Burrell Collection was eventually opened to the public, in Pollok Country Park, in 1983.

BUSBY, SIR MATT
(1909–1994)
Football manager

Matt Busby was born in Bellshill in Lanarkshire. He embarked upon a career as a professional footballer and played for Manchester City and Liverpool. His career as a player was solid, if unremarkable, but when he moved into football management he had taken the step that was to place him among the heroes of British Football. He took over as manager of Manchester United in 1945 and three years later, in 1948, the team had risen to become winners of the FA cup. The team followed this success by becoming league champions. Busby worked constantly at building a team of young and gifted players, fit to face the challenges of any of the major European sides. The team became known as 'The Busby Babes'.

In 1958, with hopes high that Manchester United would become the first British side to win the European Cup, tragedy struck when the team were involved in an air crash at Munich. Most of the young players were killed and Busby himself sustained serious injuries. On his recovery, he set to work with renewed determination to rebuild another team of equal calibre. In 1968, his efforts were rewarded and Manchester United was victorious in the European Cup. Matt Busby received a knighthood for his services to the sport in the same year. In 1982 he became president of Manchester United Football Club. He died in 1994.

BYRNE, JOHN
(1940–)
ARTIST AND WRITER

Byrne's ancestral background, like that of many Scots, is Irish. Born and brought up in Paisley, he attended St Mirin's Academy and went on to Glasgow School of Art, graduating in 1963. Working as a book-jacket designer, he was also experimenting with painting. From 1967 he created the persona of 'Patrick', based on his father, a 'naïve' self-taught artist whose primitive-style paintings became commercially successful. But Byrne was also interested in performance arts and he has written and directed stage and screen productions, beginning with *The Slab Boys* in 1978, based on his work experience in a Paisley carpet factory, now the first play of a tetralogy. He wrote the award-winning drama series *Tutti Frutti* for the BBC in 1987. It has been shown just once since then despite winning six BAFTAS. Byrne adapted the series into a National Theatre of Scotland stage production in 2006 and it enjoyed a sell-out tour. Primarily an artist, he became an associate of the Royal Scottish Academy in 2004. His works in the National Portrait Gallery include portraits of Tilda Swinton (with whom he has two sons and shares a home in Nairn), Robbie Coltrane and Billy Connolly.

CARLYLE, THOMAS
(1795–1881)
Writer and Historian

Born in Ecclefechan, Dumfriesshire, where the family home is now a museum, Carlyle was encouraged by his parents (his father was a stonemason) to pursue his education. He went to Annan Academy and Edinburgh University. At first intending to be a minister, he abandoned that for teaching but found the work, at Kirkcaldy Grammar School, intolerable, and went back to Edinburgh to study law but found that equally uncongenial. Employment as a private tutor to a bright teenager, Charles Buller, was preferable, and enabled Carlyle to embark on his true career as a 'man of letters'. Intensely interested in German literature, he translated Goethe and wrote a life of Schiller. In 1826 he married Jane Welsh, daughter of a Haddington doctor, and they settled in Edinburgh, then on her family's small estate, Craigenputtock, near Dumfries. In 1833–34 Carlyle's novel *Sartor Resartus, 'The Tailor Re-clothed'*, a satirical work whose forceful, exclamatory style was unlike anything else in English, was published in serial form. They moved to London in 1834, living in a house at Cheyne Row, Chelsea (also now a Carlyle museum).

Carlyle wrote major works on *The French Revolution* (1837) and *Frederick the Great* (1858–65). *Sartor* appeared in book form in 1838. By 1840 he was established as a pungent, acute and controversial commentator on contemporary life and letters. His wife's death in 1866 plunged him into agonies of remorse for his neglectful and irritable attitude to her. In that year he was also elected Rector of Edinburgh University. Carlyle was immensely influential in his day, and no-one can properly understand 19th-century ideas and attitudes without reading him. He died in London and is buried at Ecclefechan.

CARNEGIE, ANDREW
(1835–1919)
MILLIONAIRE AND PHILANTHROPIST

Andrew Carnegie was born in the town of Dunfermline. His father William was a weaver and in 1948 the family emigrated to the United States, settling in Pittsburgh. Andrew's first job was as a bobbin boy in a cotton mill, after which he found employment in a telegraph office. From this starting point he moved on to become a telegrapher and private secretary in the Pennsylvania Railroad Company in 1853. He was bright, hard-working and ambitious and he soon advanced within the company to become an executive.

While working with the company, he invested money in a variety of prospects, including the railways and the oil industry, and his gambles paid off, making him a wealthy man. During the American Civil War, Carnegie worked for the government, organising railway transport and telegraph services. When the war was over in 1865, he set up an ironworks and then a steel mill in Pittsburgh. The business grew to become the largest iron and steelworks in the USA and by the end of the nineteenth century, Carnegie was responsible for a quarter of America's total iron and steel production. When he sold the company in 1901, his profits ran into several millions.

Carnegie was a daring and committed capitalist, but he was also a man with an unshakeable belief in the value of education and he determined to use some of his wealth for the benefit of others. Whether his motives were entirely altruistic or had some degree of self-congratulation or self-promotion, the extent of his philanthropy was breathtaking. He set up educational trusts all over the United States and in Britain, made donations to several universities and founded almost three thousand libraries for the people on both sides of the Atlantic. He also provided funds for various new institutions, including the Peace Palace in the Hague, the foundation of the Pittsburgh Carnegie Institute and the Washington Carnegie Institution, and made several gifts to his home town of Dunfermline, including a park.

Carnegie married his wife Louise when he was 52 and they had one daughter. He bought the estate of Skibo in Sutherland for his retiral and died in Massachusetts.

CHARLES I (CHARLES STEWART)
(1600–1649)

KING OF ENGLAND, SCOTLAND, WALES AND IRELAND

Charles Stewart, the second son of James VI of Scotland (later James I of England) and Anne of Denmark, was born at Dunfermline and was the last king to be born in Scotland. Charles was a frail child, and when his older brother Henry died in 1612, making him his father's successor, there was great consternation. Charles was made Prince of Wales in 1616. In 1623, James's attempt to improve relations with Spain by securing a Spanish princess as wife for Charles met with failure. Charles married the French princess Henrietta Maria shortly after coming to the throne in 1625. The marriage was unpopular among the Puritans, as the princess was permitted to practise Roman Catholicism and raise her children in her own faith.

When Charles came to the throne, he was very much under the influence of his adviser the Duke of Buckingham, who was universally hated in England. Charles's attempts to wage war on France and Spain from 1625 to 1630 were fruitless and costly. The monarchy was in desperate financial straits and when parliament refused to grant Charles more money, he dismissed them and imposed a series of taxes and fines on his subjects. In 1628, still hampered by lack of finance, he summoned parliament and agreed to accept the Petition of Right in return for additional funds. In that same year, the Duke of Buckingham was murdered. One year later, frustrated by continual clashes with parliament, Charles dismissed them again, this time for eleven years, resorting to his former methods of raising revenue by taxation. Hostility against him grew, both in England and in Scotland, where, with the support of Archbishop Laud, his attempts to unify the faiths of the two countries by introducing *The Book of Common Prayer* sparked outright rebellion, the Covenanter's revolt. Charles's sense of insecurity increased until in 1640, with the army of the Covenant occupying the north of England, he was obliged to recall parliament. He was forced to sign the Act of Attainment, thereby losing the right to dismiss parliament without their consent, and in 1641, he was made to agree to the impeachment and execution of his loyal chancellor, the Earl of Stafford. Charles's efforts to raise support from the Scots nobility against the Puritan extremists were unsuccessful and parliament began to exercise its new powers with devastating effect.

In 1642, Civil War broke out. Three years of bitter fighting between Royalist troops and the parliament-backed forces, supported by the Scots, ensued. In 1646 Royalist forces suffered a resounding defeat at the Battle of Naseby. Charles surrendered to the Scots in 1647 and the Scots handed him over to parliament.

Growing unease among some of the Scots at the rise of Cromwell's New Model Army restored some strength to the Royalist side in the second phase of the Civil War, but it was not enough. After a further defeat of his supporters at Preston, Charles was put on trial by Cromwell's Rump Parliament. He was executed on January 30th, 1649.

Charles's life had been dogged by religious and political upheaval. His attempts to assert the powers that he believed he should have as king, against an increasingly powerful force of Puritan extremists, had only compounded his difficulties. His desire to unify the churches of Scotland and England had merely unified strength of feeling against him. He was the only king to have been executed by his own people.

CLARK, JAMES (JIM)
(1936–1968)
MOTOR-RACING DRIVER

Jim Clark was born in Kilmany, Fife. The family moved to a farm in Chirnside in Berwickshire when he was six years old and Jim attended the prestigious Loretto School in Musselburgh. His love of fast cars began at an early age and he took up motor racing when he was twenty years old, taking part in local race gatherings. His first real race was at Crimond Airfield near Aberdeen. The first race he won was in 1956, and in 1958 and 1959 he won the title of Scottish Speed Champion. Later, in 1960, he took part in his first Grand Prix, driving a Lotus for Colin Chapman's team. He was to remain with the Lotus team for the rest of his career. In 1961, he took his first Grand Prix title at Pau in France. It was to be the first of a series of successes in a remarkable career, including a record-breaking total of twenty-five Grand Prix wins, five of which were in Great Britain. In 1963, a year in which he won seven Grand Prix races, he earned a place in the record books when he became the youngest driver so far to win the World Championship. He won the title again two years later, in 1965, and in the same year he drove to victory in the Indianapolis 500, the first non-American to do so.

In only eight years, he had become a legend in the motor racing world. His career looked set to continue in the same vein, but tragically he was killed in 1968 in a high-speed accident, during practice for a race in Hockenheim in Germany. His body was returned to his home town of Chirnside for burial and the world of motor racing was left stunned, wondering what might have been.

The Jim Clark Trophy Room in Newtown Street, Duns in the Scottish Borders houses a collection of awards and trophies donated by Clark's parents, and is open to the public at specified times

COCHRANE, THOMAS, 10TH EARL OF DUNDONALD
(1775–1860)
NAVAL OFFICER AND REFORMIST POLITICIAN

Cochrane is the model for two fictional naval heroes, Horatio Hornblower and Jack Aubrey. Born at Annsfield, Hamilton, he entered the Royal Navy at 18 and had his first command in 1800. His small vessel captured a 32-gun French frigate. Briefly captured by the French, he was exchanged and promoted to the rank of Post-Captain. Excelling at capture, he made a substantial fortune in prize-money. In 1808, with a small force, he defended the almost untenable fort of Rosas on the Spanish coast, and in 1809 was knighted for his action against the French fleet in Aix Roads. Though a dashing officer, he often antagonised his superiors. His political views were strongly reformist and he entered parliament in 1806 as member for Honiton, then for Westminster. Corruption in the Navy was his great target. In 1814 he was himself found guilty of financial corruption in what was almost certainly a frame-up. Imprisoned for a year, struck off the Navy list, deprived of his knighthood, he was expelled from parliament but re-elected by Westminster. He then led the naval forces of Chile and Brazil in their successful wars of independence, and also tried to set up an independent Greek navy. In 1831 he succeeded to the earldom and in 1832 was granted a free pardon and gazetted a Rear-Admiral. He was buried in Westminster Abbey.

COLLINS, WILLIAM
(1789–1853)
BOOK PUBLISHER

William Collins was born in Eastwood, Renfrewshire. His first job was as a clerk in a cotton mill. He was a religious young man with a powerful social conscience and a strong belief in the value of education and he gave up his spare time to hold classes for the workers. In 1813, he opened up an independent school in Glasgow for the education of the poor.

As a member of the congregation at the Tron Church in Glasgow, Collins made the acquaintance of Thomas

Chalmers the evangelist, and the two became friends. William met Thomas's brother Charles Chalmers and in partnership with Charles, he started a business in 1819, publishing and selling books. Many of the books that were published by Collins were school textbooks, and another large proportion of the books religious texts. A teetotaller and committed member of the Temperance Movement, William also produced several temperance publications, including *The Temperance Society Record*, which he wrote himself.

The Collins publishing company grew from strength to strength and was to become the largest independent publishing house in Britain. William's son, also called William, became involved in the business when he was very young and on the death of his father, took over control, expanding the firm and establishing it as a major publisher of bibles. The firm which William Collins Senior had begun remained in the control of the family until 1979 when the family sold out to Rupert Murdoch. In 1989 there was an amalgamation of Collins, Harper and Row, Gower Publishing *inter alia* and in 1990 Harper Collins became a worldwide company name.

COLUMBA, SAINT
(521–597)
MISSIONARY AND FOUNDER OF CHRISTIANITY IN SCOTLAND

Saint Columba, also known as Colum or Columcille, was born at Gartan, Donegal in Ireland. Both his parents were of royal descent. He studied at Clonard under St

Finnan. In 546, Columba founded a church at Derry, now the town of Londonderry, and he also founded a monastery at Durrow where he lived and worked as a scholar, transcribing and decorating religious writings. In 563, having been excommunicated and banished for his part in a battle at Cuildreimhne, he set out in a small boat with twelve disciples and sailed to Iona. On the island of Iona he founded a monastery and began the task of converting the people of Scotland to Christianity. He travelled with his missionaries around the north of Scotland and preached Christianity to the Pictish tribes, winning the respect of those whom he sought to convert and those whom he led. The monastery on Iona was the base from which he worked, training his missionaries to go forth and spread the word of God. It served as the mother church from which all the other churches that sprang up round Scotland took their lead. Many churches were founded on the mainland and in the Hebrides. After thirty-four years in Scotland, Columba died and was buried on Iona, but after his death the mark of his influence could be seen in monasteries and churches all over the north of the country and as far south as the north of England.

CONNERY, SEAN (THOMAS)
(1930–)
ACTOR

Thomas Connery was born in Fountainbridge in Edinburgh. His father was a truck driver and the family were far from wealthy. He joined the Royal Navy after leaving school, but was discharged on medical grounds. Then followed a succession of jobs, which included spells as milkman, lifeguard, undertaker's assistant and model for life-drawing classes. When he was twenty-three, Connery's muscular build and masculine good looks – and a place as runner-up in the British heats of Mr Universe – helped him to secure a part in the chorus of the stage production of South Pacific, which was playing in London at the time. His acting career was only moderately successful at first. He made his first appearance on television in 1956 and in the late 1950s appeared in a number of MGM films. His first major role was in *Another Time, Another Place* in 1958.

In 1962, Connery was offered the role of James Bond in *Dr No*. The film was a huge success, establishing Connery as a star of the big screen and leading to four further Bond movies in the next five years; From *Russia With Love* (1963), *Goldfinger* (1964), *Thunderball* (1965) and *You Only Live Twice* (1967). In those years he also appeared in four other films; *Marnie* (1964), *Woman of Straw* (1964), *The Hill* (1965) and *A Fine Madness* (1966), but to the British cinema-going public he was first and foremost Bond. In order to shake off this image, Connery stepped back from the Bond role for four years, working on other projects on screen. He returned as Bond in 1972 in *Diamonds are Forever* and in 1983 made his final appearance as the spy in *Never Say Never Again*.

Although he is most famous for his part in the Bond movies, Connery has given memorable performances in several other major films and has established himself as a versatile and gifted actor in a wide variety of roles. Some of the best-known of these include *The Man Who Would Be King* (1975) in which he co-starred with Michael Caine, *Murder on the Orient Express* (1974), *A Bridge Too Far* (1977), *The Untouchables* (1987), for which he won the Academy Award for Best Supporting Actor, *The Name of the Rose* (1987), *The Hunt for Red October* (1990), *Entrapment* (1999), and *The League of Extraordinary Gentlemen* (2003).

Connery has lived with his wife Micheline in Spain for many years, but retains a strong sense of national pride and he is a loyal supporter of the Scottish National Party. His home city of Edinburgh awarded him the freedom of the city in 1991. He was knighted by the Queen in July 2000 at the Palace of Holyroodhouse in Edinburgh. Sir Sean has also been awarded the Legion d'Honneur, France's highest decoration and is a Commandeur des Arts et des Lettres.

CONNOLLY, BILLY
(1942–)
COMEDIAN AND ACTOR

Billy Connolly was born in Anderston in Glasgow. He attended St Gerard's Secondary School and then worked as a baker's delivery boy before taking up an apprenticeship as a welder in the shipyards. Billy played the banjo and in the 1960s, he toured the folk circuit playing and singing with Gerry Rafferty in the Humblebums. But it was as a stand-up comedian that he was to make his name as 'The Big Yin'. His outrageous dress sense on stage and his equally outrageous banter won him a following nationwide. In the 1970s, his shows were a sellout and recordings of his performances proved popular with his fans. Appearances on television chat shows such as *Parkinson* showed that Connolly had a capacity for being as funny in conversation as he was on stage, having a gift for seeing the ridiculous in the everyday situations with which all of his audience were familiar.

The late 1970s were quite difficult years; relentless work schedules, a failing marriage and alcohol problems took their toll. In 1978, he moved to London with actress and comedienne Pamela Stephenson (who is now a clinical psychologist). His popularity in the United States of America was growing and in 1988 he and Pamela moved to Los Angeles where Connolly was offered the lead role in his own sitcom, *Billy*. He returned to Scotland in 1994 to make his *World Tour of Scotland* series for television and this proved to be very successful. It was followed by his *World Tour of Australia*, *World Tour of England, Ireland and Wales* and *World Tour of New Zealand* which have been equally popular. Connolly has been involved in a number of films in his career and he won critical acclaim and a BAFTA nomination for his portrayal of Queen Victoria's ghillie, JOHN BROWN, when he co-starred with Judi Dench in the film *Mrs Brown* in 1997. He continues to perform live, although less frequently. Tickets sell out in hours.

In 1985, Connolly became involved in the massive

fund-raising effort Live Aid, which was started to provide relief for famine-stricken Ethiopia. He has also been a committed worker for Comic Relief since it was founded. In July 2001 Connolly was awarded an Honorary Doctorate from Glasgow University, and in 2003 a CBE in the Queen's birthday honours. In 2005 he and his wife returned to live in Scotland, living part of the year in Aberdeenshire and part of the year in Malta.

CONNOLLY, JAMES
(1868–1916)
Labour Leader and Irish Nationalist

Born to Irish immigrant parents in Edinburgh, Connolly joined the army in 1882 as a boy soldier, and was stationed at the Curragh Camp, outside Dublin. He deserted and returned home to marry an Irish girl. Already an avid reader of Marx and Engels, he was imbued with Socialist ideas and gained a reputation in Labour circles as an effective speaker and organiser. In 1896 he went back to Dublin to help found the Irish Socialist Republican Party. Between 1903 and 1910 he was in the USA, with his young family, lecturing to working men's groups, and was one of the founders of the International Workers of the World, an organisation intended to unite the working people of all nations against exploitation. Connolly returned to Ireland in 1910 as a union organiser and combined nationalist sentiment with his Socialist internationalism. He was one of the leaders of the 1916 'Easter Rising', whose failure provoked the campaign which led eventually to home rule and an Irish republic. Wounded in the fighting, he was propped in a chair to be executed by a firing squad. Now he is a hero of Irish liberation, but his political ideas have never found much acceptance there.

COULTHARD, DAVID
(1971–)
RACING DRIVER

Coulthard, born in Twynholm, Dumfriesshire, opened his racing career as national Junior Kart champion at the age of 12. Already sure of what he wanted to be, he progressed from karting to racing cars. In 1989 he was Maclaren Autosport Young Driver of the Year, and breaking a leg in an accident in 1990 hardly interrupted his progress. In 1993 he joined the Williams Renault racing team, first as a test driver but was soon promoted to Race Driver. His first major win was the Portuguese Grand Prix in 1995, and from then on he remained among the top ten – sometimes the top two or three – racing drivers of the world. In 1996 he joined the Maclaren Mercedes Formula One team. Coulthard was among the survivors when a private plane in which he was travelling crashed at Lyon, France, in May 2000. In 2005 he left Maclaren for Red Bull Racing, and published an autobiography, *It Is What It Is*, in 2007. He announced he would retire from active participation at the end of 2008. Coulthard married Karen Minier in 2008 and they have a son. They live in Monaco, where he is a two-times winner of the Grand Prix.

CRAMPSEY, ROBERT (BOB)
(1930–2008)
TEACHER AND BROADCASTER

Once described as a 'Scottish cultural institution', Crampsey was a polymath with a breathtaking range of ability and expertise. Born in Glasgow, he wrote an entertaining account of his youth in *The Young Civilian*. After graduation from Glasgow University he did his national service in the RAF, then became a teacher, and eventually head of St Ambrose High School, Coatbridge. He is best-known as a football commentator, having been a regular participant in the long-running STV programme *Scotsport*, and later on BBC Radio Scotland. An authority on the history of the game in Scotland, he wrote the official history of the Scottish League as well as a history of Queen's Park Rangers and a biography of Jock Stein. In 1965, Crampsey won the BBC's *Brain of Britain* competition, reflecting a range and depth of interests in subjects as diverse as Italian opera and English county cricket. In his later years, Crampsey suffered from Parkinson's Disease but remained active as a broadcaster, raconteur and writer, and a strong believer in the concept of 'life-long learning', both for himself and for others.

CUNNINGHAME GRAHAM, ROBERT BONTINE
(1852–1936)
WRITER, TRAVELLER AND POLITICIAN

Cunninghame Graham was born in London, where

the family had a home as well as in Scotland, and went to Harrow School. At the age of 17 he travelled to Argentina, became a cattle rancher and married a Chilean poetess in 1879. On inheriting the family estate in Dunbartonshire in 1883, he returned to Scotland. Despite his exotic background, he was passionately Scottish in his ideas and sympathies. Unusually for a landowner, he was strongly anti-imperialist and in favour of social reform. Elected as Liberal MP for North-West Lanarkshire in 1886, he became the first President of the newly-formed Scottish Labour Party in 1888. Later, he was prominent in the nationalist movement, becoming President of the National Party of Scotland (1928) and the Scottish National Party (1934). Always a flamboyant and often outspoken figure, 'Don Roberto' was an intrepid traveller, in North Africa as well as South America, and a writer of essays and short stories. He died in Argentina and is buried in Inchmahome Priory on the Lake of Menteith.

CUTLER, IVOR
(1923–2006)
POET AND PERFORMER

Scotland's Jewish community has produced its full share of humorists but Ivor Cutler was a unique figure, developing his own gently anarchistic, surrealistic and highly individual brand of comedy over the decades. Deceptively frail in appearance, hesitant in utterance, his manner concealed a sharp mind, strong opinions and a profound, not wholly tolerant observation of his fellow humans. Born in Ibrox, Glasgow, he parodied his early years in *Life in a Scotch Sitting Room, Vol. 2* (there is no volume one), a hilarious description of monumental gloom. In 1941 he enlisted for the RAF, but was dismissed as being too dreamy to be an aircraft navigator, and worked as a first-aid assistant and storeman. After the Second World War he studied at Glasgow School of Art and became a teacher. But the repressive discipline of Scottish schools appalled him, and he left for England, where he taught for a time at A S Neill's progressive Summerhill School. Later he worked for the Inner London Education Authority, maintaining parallel careers as teacher and entertainer. His first public show, in 1957, mystified most of his audience. But in the 1960s he began to find a warmer reception. Though never a showbiz 'regular', he appeared on programmes like *Late Night Line-Up* and was invited by Paul McCartney to perform in the Beatles' film *Magical Mystery Tour* (1967). Gradually he gained a public who enjoyed his quirkiness, occasional gruffness and comic resource. He lived in London, enjoying its variety, and learning Chinese so that he could talk to the locals in Chinatown, Soho. His relationship with his native country was always slightly barbed. Imbued with Scottish culture, tradition, and attitudes, he fought them, mocked them, but wryly agreed that they were, whether he liked it or not, part of him.

DALE, DAVID
(1739–1806)
ENTREPRENEUR AND SOCIAL REFORMER

With a family background in the linen trade, Dale was born in Stewarton, Ayrshire and trained for the textile business. In 1778 he set up Scotland's first cotton mill, at Rothesay, and in 1785, with Joseph Arkwright, began the development of the mills at New Lanark, in the steep valley just below the Falls of Clyde. Dale was an enlightened and philanthropic owner for his time, and the New Lanark community had far more facilities for employees and their children's welfare and education than was usual. By 1795 over 1300 people worked at New Lanark. In 1799, Dale sold his interest in New Lanark to his son-in-law, the Welshman Robert Owen, who shared and developed many of Dale's ideas. The community, with its terraced houses, schools, church, and imposing factory blocks, still remains as a 'world heritage site' much as Dale built it. He retired to Glasgow, where he led a Presbyterian sect known as The Old Scotch Independents.

DALGLISH, KENNETH MATHIESON (KENNY)
(1951–)
FOOTBALL PLAYER AND MANAGER

Kenny Dalglish was born in Glasgow and at the age of seventeen, signed up with Celtic, then managed by Jock Stein. He remained with Celtic for ten years, a period in which he won every award in Scottish football. In 1977, he was transferred, for a record-breaking fee, to Liverpool. His success with the Scottish team was repeated with the English one. He won every award in the English game, and played a part in Liverpool's victories in three European Cups. He played for the Scottish international side and was capped 102 times. As a player, he was not only skilful, but consistent and, remaining reasonably injury-free, also reliable. He became the first player to have scored 100 goals in both Scottish and English football and he also scored a record 30 goals for his national side.

From player, Dalglish progressed to manager and took over at Liverpool in 1985 while he was still playing for the team. His success in this double role surprised and delighted even the cynics. That same year, Liverpool won both the League and the FA Cup. He moved from Liverpool six years later to take over at Blackburn Rovers where he spent four successful years as manager. Shortly after Blackburn's victory in the Premier League in 1994 to 1995, Dalglish moved to Newcastle United. In 1999, he returned to Scotland as Director of Football Operations at Celtic. He was sacked from this job in 2000, but won compensation for unfair dismissal.

In 2004, Kenny and his wife Marina founded The Marina Dalglish Appeal to raise money for breast cancer research. The whole family have participated in fundraising. Marina Dalglish was awarded an MBE in the 2009 New Year's Honours list.

DOYLE, SIR ARTHUR CONAN

(1859–1930)

DOCTOR, AUTHOR

Arthur Conan Doyle was born in Edinburgh. He was educated at Stonyhurst College and then was accepted into Edinburgh University to study medicine. During his university days, he had his first story published in *Chambers' Journal* in 1879. Doyle spent some months working first as a ship's surgeon on a whaler and then on a liner sailing to Africa. Finally he set up in practice in Southsea where financial struggles prompted him to turn his hand to writing again to boost incoming funds.

A Study in Scarlet, published in 1887, introduced the characters of the brilliant private detective Sherlock Holmes and his admiring sidekick Dr Watson which were to become firm favourites with Doyle's reading public. A second short novel, *A Sign of Four*, appeared in 1890, and from 1891 to 1893 a series of short stories featuring Holmes appeared in *Strand Magazine*.

An attempt to kill his hero off at the hands of the arch-villain Moriarty was met with such an outcry that Doyle was forced to resurrect Holmes a few years later. In addition to the series of short stories, *The Adventures of Sherlock Holmes*, *The Memoirs of Sherlock Holmes* and *The Return of Sherlock Holmes*, Doyle wrote a longer book featuring Holmes, *The Hound of the Baskervilles*, in 1892.

It is undoubtedly the creation of Holmes that earned

Doyle his reputation as a popular writer, and the detective has featured in several dramatic productions on stage and screen in the years since he was first dreamed up. However, Doyle wrote several other books that he considered to be of greater importance. These include *Micah Clarke* (1887), *The White Company* (1890), *Brigadier Gerard* (1896) and *Rodney Stone* (1896).

During the Second Boer War, Doyle served as a military physician and was awarded a knighthood in 1902 for his writing on the subject, *The War in South Africa*. In 1909, he played a vital role in helping to secure the release of Oscar Slater, imprisoned for several years on a wrongful charge of murder. During the First World War, Doyle worked as a war correspondent. He died in retiral in Sussex.

DUNBAR, WILLIAM
(*c*.1460–*c*.1515)
POET

For a great poet, little is known about Dunbar's life. Probably born in East Lothian, he studied at St Andrews University between 1475–79, then became a member of the Franciscan Order and travelled in England and northern France. He may have been a secretary or clerk to some of the diplomatic missions sent by James IV to European courts, and from 1501 was recipient of a royal pension, which rose over the years from £10 to £80. That year, he visited England in connection with plans for the wedding of James IV to Margaret Tudor, which inspired his poem 'The Thrissil and the Rois', of

1503. He mixed in court circles, writing a wide variety of verse from sacred hymns to diversions and satires, as well as his powerful, sometimes scabrous major poems like 'The Dance of the Sevin Deidly Sinnis' and 'The Twa Marriit Wemen and the Wedo', and the famous 'Lament for the Makaris', enumerating the poets who are no more, and anticipating Dunbar's own demise with 'Timor mortis conturbat me'. In 1508, seven of his poems were printed by Walter Chepman, the first example of Scottish typography. Dunbar was always hoping for a lucrative Church post, but he never got one. His name is not recorded after 1515, and he may have been a victim of the defeat at Flodden.

DUNLOP, JOHN BOYD
(1840–1921)
INVENTOR OF THE PNEUMATIC TYRE

John Boyd Dunlop was born in Dreghorn, Ayrshire. He studied to become a veterinary surgeon and worked in practice in Edinburgh for a short period before moving to Ireland and settling in Belfast in 1867.

Some years later, he fitted a set of home-made tyres to his child's tricycle using lengths of rubber hosepipe inflated with air and realising the potential of his idea, he started up a business in 1889 to produce pneumatic tyres, firstly for bicycles, and then for motor cars. A considerable improvement on the old solid rubber tyres, the pneumatic tyres were an outstanding commercial success and the Dunlop Rubber Company grew from strength to strength. Although John Dunlop was the man who developed the idea into a business and has been widely credited as the inventor of the pneumatic tyre, a patent had been produced some years beforehand, in 1845, by another Scot, an engineer called Robert William Thomson.

DUNNET, DOROTHY
(1923–2001)
NOVELIST

Born Dorothy Halliday in Dunfermline, she attended James Gillespie's High School for Girls in Edinburgh, at the same time as another novelist-to-be, Muriel Spark. Her first job was as Press Officer for the Scottish Office, in 1940. It brought her in contact with journalists, and she married one, Alastair Dunnet, in 1946. Dunnet's creative powers were first revealed by her talent for portrait painting, and she exhibited at several Royal Scottish Academy shows. In the late 1950s, she began writing fiction, with the aim of producing the kind of historical novel she would have liked to read herself – a blend of accurate period detail, dramatic action, high culture, rich description, and humour that transformed a somewhat tired genre into something new and appealing. Turned down by five British publishers, *Game of Kings* was first published in the USA (1961), but soon also appeared in Britain. It heralded fifteen years of writing her sequence of the six *Lymond Chronicles*, interspersed with detective tales. She followed this up with, the eight-volume *House of Niccolò* series, but nearest to her heart was *King Hereafter* (1982), a novel based on the life of Macbeth and pursuing her theory (not widely accepted) that Macbeth and his historical contemporary the half-viking Earl Thorfinn of Orkney, were one and the same person. She was involved in Edinburgh's literary life, particularly with the National Library of Scotland, and the Edinburgh Book Festival.

FERGUSON, SIR ALEX
(1941–)
FOOTBALL PLAYER AND MANAGER

Alex Ferguson was born in Govan, Glasgow and worked as an apprentice toolmaker. He played football at amateur level for Queen's Park Rangers in 1957, and in 1964 turned professional and played in turn for Dunfermline, Glasgow Rangers, Falkirk and Ayr. When his playing days were over, he moved into management and proved himself a gifted leader.

He worked at East Stirling for a few months, then moved to St Mirren in 1974. After joining Aberdeen in 1978, he led the team to victory in the Scottish League Championship. This triumph was repeated twice more and from 1978 to 1986, Aberdeen also won the Scottish Cup four times, the European Cup Winners Cup and the Super Cup in 1983. He acted as manager for Scotland for a short spell and then moved on to take charge at Manchester United in 1986.

His career at Manchester United has been marked with outstanding success, and the team have won all the major awards in English football, including the double (the FA cup and the League cup) twice. In 1999, the highest point of Ferguson's career was reached when Manchester United won the European Cup final, securing the treble – FA, League and European cups – an outstanding achievement both for Ferguson and his players. Alex Ferguson's contribution to British football was recognised when he was awarded a knighthood in July 1999.

FINLAY, IAN HAMILTON
(1925–2006)
CONCEPTUAL ARTIST

In 2004, a poll of artists and arts experts voted Little Sparta to be the most important work of art in Scotland. Its creator was born at Nassau, Bahamas in 1925, and was brought home as a child, becoming a pupil at Dollar Academy. In the Second World War he joined the Army Service Corps. He became friends with Hugh MacDiarmid, who was best man at his wedding to Marion Fletcher in 1945; they subsequently became enemies, then were reconciled in the 1970s. Finlay published *The Sea-Bed and Other Stories* and a poetry collection, *The Dancers Inherit the Party*, in the 1950s. In 1961 he set up the Wild Hawthorn Press in Edinburgh and also a poetry magazine, *Poor. Old. Tired. Horse.* With *Rapel* (1963) he became the leading British exponent of 'concrete' verse, where the shape and typography are intrinsic to the poem. But he was already moving into conceptual art – where the artist supplies an idea, or metaphor, and others collaborate in its making. In 1964 he married for the second time, and with his wife Sue Macdonald-Lockhart bought the derelict farm of

Stonypath, Lanarkshire, and began to turn it into a work of art – a garden which has been described as 'an aesthetic adventure', rich in symbolism, verbal and visual puns, motifs that contrast with or complement one another, all executed with meticulous cratfsmanship, adding up to a highly complex, deeply-memorable experience for the visitor-explorer. For a pacifist, Finlay had a combative nature: the name Little Sparta epitomised his attitude to the arts bureaucrats of the 'Athens of the North'; he also battled with the local council. Belatedly his achievement was recognised with a CBE and a 'Creative Scotland' award from the Arts Council (2003). He had long been a celebrity in the art world outside Scotland.

FLEMING, ALEXANDER
(1881–1955)
Doctor, discoverer of penicillin

Alexander Fleming was born in Ayrshire. His first job was as a shipping clerk, but in 1902 he embarked upon his medical studies in London at St Mary's Medical School. He was a brilliant student and qualified in both medicine and surgery. He remained at St Mary's after his qualification and began work in the research laboratory under Sir Almroth Wright. There, he pioneered the use of antityphoid vaccines on human beings and also the use of salvarsan in combating syphilitic infection.

Fleming served as a medical officer during the First World War and was appalled to see how many soldiers died as a result of wound infection, rather than from the wounds themselves. This was a motivating factor behind much of the work which led to the discovery of penicillin.

In 1921, Fleming discovered lysosome, a substance present in human mucous and tears, which was capable of dissolving some common bacteriae. Its clinical applications were, however, limited. Then in 1928, he discovered, quite by chance, that mould on a dirty petrie dish had dissolved a culture of staphylococci. Further investigation revealed that the same mould was active against several other disease-causing bacteriae, including streptococcus, pneumococcus and gonococcus. Fleming wrote a paper on his findings and continued his investigations, but the mould, penicillium notatum, was difficult to produce in large enough quantities and in a form pure enough for clinical use. He eventually abandoned his work on the project in 1930, to concentrate on other aspects of research. Eleven years later, two scientists from Oxford University, Howard Florey and Ernst Chain, took up the work that Fleming had begun and were successful in developing a method of obtaining penicillin that was suitable for large-scale production. Manufacturers in the United States were very swift to start producing penicillin during World War II, and very soon the drug was proving itself to be an invaluable tool in the fight against a broad spectrum of bacterial infections, saving the lives of hundreds of fighting men.

Fleming was appointed Professor of Bacteriology at London in 1938 and was knighted in 1944. Fleming,

Florey and Chain were awarded the Nobel prize for Medicine in 1945. Although the drug might never have come into clinical use without the work of Florey and Chain, it is generally Fleming who is remembered for the discovery of penicillin.

FORSYTH, WILLIAM DAVID (BILL)
(1947–)
Film Maker

Reading, rather than cinema-going, was the main influence on the young Forsyth as he grew up in his native Glasgow. As a teenager his first job was with the Thames and Clyde Film Production Company, making short documentaries and promotional films, and his ambition to make a feature film was not realised until 1979, when *That Sinking Feeling* was produced with the Glasgow Youth Theatre, on a tiny budget. Its success led to *Gregory's Girl* (1981) and *Local Hero* (1983). Forsyth's achievements on shoestring budgets led to the establishment of the Scottish Film Production Fund in 1983, but he himself went to the USA in 1986. He made *Housekeeping* (1987), *Breaking In* (1989) and *Being Human* (1993) but found the commercial demands of American film making restrictive and returned somewhat disillusioned after fifteen years to make another film in Scotland, *Gregory's Two Girls* (1999), a sequel to his first big success.

His work, often dealing with life's uncertainties, anguish and alienation, laid the foundations which a new generation of film makers has built on.

FULTON, RIKKI

(1924–2004)

COMEDIAN, ACTOR AND ENTERTAINER

Rikki Fulton was born in Glasgow. His career as an actor, comedian and variety performer spanned more than fifty years, during which he enjoyed enduring popularity in the theatre and on television.

He began working for the BBC in the 1950s and appeared in a variety of programmes, including drama and children's productions. His theatrical career was equally diverse. Repertory appearances in the early days led to major roles in variety shows, notably *The Five Past Eight Show* which was produced in both Edinburgh and Glasgow.

Over the years he became well-loved for the various comic characters he played on stage and television, including his double act with Jack Milroy as Francie and Josie, and his portrayal of the lugubrious minister, the Reverend IM Jolly, who sprang from his own television sketch show, *Scotch and Wry*. Fulton also proved to be a hilarious pantomime dame and appeared in this capacity from his early days in the performing profession.

In addition to his comedy work on stage and television, he appeared in the films *Gorky Park*, *Local Hero*, *Comfort and Joy*, and *The Girl in the Picture* and proved that he had an undoubted talent for straight acting.

He received an honorary doctorate from St Andrews University in 2000. In his latter years he suffered from Alzheimer's disease, first showing symptoms in 1998 and finally being diagnosed in 2002. He died in 2004. His wife Kate Matheson, who wrote the book *Rikki & Me,* died in 2005.

Fulton was one of the most influential and well-loved entertainers Scotland has ever produced.

GARDEN, MARY
(1874–1967)
Opera singer

Mary Garden, originally Mary Davidson, was born in Aberdeen but was taken by her father, a wealthy businessman, to live in America at the age of six. It was there that she began to train as a singer and her studies took her from Chicago to Paris. Her singing debut was unexpected and quite astounding. The singer of the title role in Charpentier's *Louise* was taken ill during a performance at the Opéra Comique and Mary was obliged to take her place.

Mary's career moved swiftly on from that point. In 1902, at the request of the composer, Claude Débussy, she created the role of Mélisande in the opera *Pélleas et Mélisande*. She also recorded songs with the composer and her name was at one point linked with him romantically. Her success took her to Covent Garden in 1902 to 1903 and she sang, to great acclaim, a variety of roles including Carmen, Juliet, Manon and Salomé. She returned to America in 1907 and soon afterwards became principal soprano with the Chicago Grand Opera. She remained with the Chicago Grand Opera for more than twenty years. After a brief spell in

Hollywood, she returned to Paris in the late 1930s, but as World War II took its grip she returned to Scotland and to Aberdeen.

Although she was said to have had close associations with various prominent men during her professional life, Mary Garden never married. She made her permanent home in Aberdeen in her later life, but travelled to America from time to time after the war was over, to visit or to give lectures.

She died in Aberdeen, aged 93.

GIBBON, LEWIS GRASSIC
See Mitchell, James Leslie

GLENNIE, EVELYN
(1965–)
SOLO PERCUSSIONIST

Evelyn Glennie was born in Aberdeen. Her musical ability was obvious from an early age and she began studying timpani and percussion at the age of twelve. In 1982, she was accepted into the Royal Academy of Music in London. Her gift for music, her dedication and sheer hard work ensured that she graduated with many prizes, including the Queen's Commendation for All Round Excellence, the highest accolade offered by the college. A scholarship award in 1986 allowed her to travel to Japan to broaden her musical horizons with further study. Evelyn's career has never known a lull since her graduation. Standing alone as a full-time solo percussionist of unparalleled ability, she is in demand as a performer worldwide and every year sees her taking part in an concert schedule that involves travel to every corner of the globe. Appearances on television and radio broadcasts have brought her music to a wider audience than the concert-going public and her energy and enthusiasm, coupled with her brilliant performance, make her a very charismatic figure on screen. She has done much to popularise classical music and reach many people who might never have considered themselves music lovers at all, but is also committed to studying a wide variety of musical cultures and putting what she has learnt before her audience.

She plays a vast array of percussion instruments, both manufactured and home-made, and also plays the highland pipes. Several composers have written concertos and recital pieces to add to Evelyn's solo percussion repertoire. She is also an accomplished composer herself. Amongst the many honours that Evelyn has received, she has been a Fellow of the Royal College of Music and of the Royal Academy of Music. She was voted Scots Woman of the Decade in 1990 and was awarded an OBE in 1993. Glennie has been awarded honorary degrees from many British universities.

Although Evelyn Glennie has been profoundly deaf since the age of twelve, she believes that her deafness is not an issue as far as her musicianship is concerned.

GLOVER, THOMAS
(1838–1911)
'The Scottish Samurai'

Thomas Glover, the son of a coastguard officer, was

born in Fraserburgh and educated in Aberdeen. When he was nineteen, he travelled to Shanghai to begin working for Jardine, Matheson and company, a large trading business. Two years later, he moved to Japan, to the newly opened trading port of Nagasaki, where he took up the post of clerk to Kenneth MacKenzie, agent of Jardine, Matheson and Co. At that time trading in Japan, which was under the control of the shogun, was difficult and dangerous for foreigners, but Glover mastered the language and established himself as a successful trader, taking over as sole agent for Jardine, Matheson and Co. after the departure of MacKenzie two years later. He started trading in tea and diversified into silk, fabrics, and gold. Then as rebellion amongst the samurai against the shogun broke out, he began importing arms to assist the rebels in their cause. He played an important but clandestine role in the rebellion until 1868, when the rule of the shogun collapsed and the emperor was reinstated.

After the war was over, Glover struggled in the punishing economic depression that followed in spite of all that he had achieved so far. He had become a successful trader in ships and had arranged for the import of three Scottish-built warships to Japan, contributing significantly to the growth of the new navy in the emerging power. He had arranged for the shipping to Nagasaki of Japan's first slip-dock for shipbuilding. He owned a coalmine in Takashima. But he ran into a string of financial problems and his company collapsed in 1870, leaving him bankrupt. He worked in management at the mine for the next six years, paying off his debts. Then he moved to Tokyo to act as adviser to Yatoro Iwasaki, founder of Mitsubishi, a rapidly expanding shipping and shipbuilding concern. Glover had friendly contacts in the Japanese government and experience in trading overseas which would be of immense value to the company. In 1881 the Mitsubishi company bought the Takashima mine and Glover returned to Nagasaki to oversee its commercial running. At this time he became Portuguese consul in Nagasaki and Mitsubishi bought over Glover's slip-dock in Nagasaki.

Mitsubishi expanded further and shipyards in Honshu were purchased. Then in 1885 Glover founded the Japan Brewery Company and moved to Yokohama. Dubbed 'The Scottish Samurai' because of the part he played in the downfall of the shogun, Glover held an esteemed position in Japanese society, in recognition of his contributions to the building of the new Japan. He moved amongst the most important dignitaries in politics and commerce. In 1908 he was presented with the Order of the Rising Sun, second class. When he died in 1911, he was cremated in Tokyo and his ashes were buried in Nagasaki.

GRAHAM, JAMES, 5TH EARL AND 1ST MARQUIS OF MONTROSE
(1612–1650)
NOBLEMAN AND SOLDIER

Montrose was born in Kincardine Castle and attended

the University of St Andrews. After spending some time travelling in Europe, he returned to Scotland in 1637. It was a time of religious strife, when the Presbyterians of Scotland were resisting the attempts of Charles I to bring them into line with the Church of England. Montrose was one of the four Scottish nobles who drew up the National Covenant at Greyfriars in Edinburgh. He took part in the first Bishop's War on the side of the Covenanters, and occupied the city of Aberdeen, but following the conciliation at Berwick, Montrose began to have doubts about his allegiance. He expressed his opposition to the proposed union between the Covenanters and the English Puritan army, and was imprisoned for a period in Edinburgh Castle in 1643, until Charles secured his release.

Montrose, now the Marquis of Montrose and the King's Lieutenant in Scotland, set out in 1644 to rally support in the Highlands for Charles. He fought successfully in six battles at Tippermuir, Aberdeen, Inverlochy, Auldearn, Alford and Kilsyth from 1644 to 1645. However, his attempt to continue the struggle further south was frustrated when his forces suffered defeat at Philiphaugh in 1645. In 1646, the king was captured and Montrose was forced to take flight to Norway. When news reached him of the execution of Charles I in 1649, he determined to avenge his king and returned to Scotland. However, he lost the greater part of his fighting force in a shipwreck off Orkney and after suffering defeat at Carbisdale in 1650, he became a fugitive once more. Betrayed by McLeod of Assynt, he was taken to Edinburgh and executed without trial in May the same year. The bravery he had shown throughout his struggle to defend the monarchy did not desert him and he faced his death with great courage.

GRAHAME, KENNETH
(1859–1932)
Author

Kenneth Grahame was born in Edinburgh, where his father worked as a lawyer. Grahame attended St Edward's School in Oxford and lived in London for a brief period before starting work as a clerk with the Bank of England in 1879. He started writing some years later and his early work consisted of short stories and essays. In 1893, his first collection of work, *Pagan Papers*, was published and this was followed by *The Golden Age* in 1895 and *Dream Days* in 1898, both of which proved to be very successful. In 1898, Grahame was promoted to secretary of the Bank of England and he married one year later. He continued to write and in 1908, the same year in which he felt obliged to retire from the bank on account of his ill-health, his most successful and best-loved children's book, *The Wind in the Willows*, was published. The book had its origins in a number of stories that Grahame had written for his son, and it featured the charming and unforgettable characters of Mole, Ratty and Toad in a beautifully written set of riverside adventures. The book, now accepted as a children's classic, has an enduring appeal not only for its youthful readers, but also for the adult reading public. Children's writer AA Milne wrote a dramatised version of *The Wind in the Willows*, published in 1929, called *Toad of Toad Hall*. Grahame died in 1932.

GRAY, ALASDAIR
(1934–)
Writer and Artist

Born in Riddrie, East Glasgow, Gray spent his early years there. From 1940–42 he was evacuated with his mother and sister to Auchterarder, Perthshire, then to Stonehouse, Lanarkshire. The family then lived for four years in Wetherby, Yorkshire, before returning to Glasgow, where Alasdair attended Whitehill Senior Secondary School, and then Glasgow School of Art. He gained a diploma in design and mural painting. He worked on various commissions as a mural painter, taught art, became a scene painter and was frequently out of paid work, though still busy both as a writer of prose and verse and a painter. From 1960 he has also been an ardent campaigner against nuclear weapons. In 1961 he married Inge Sørensen, with whom he had a son in 1964. That year he also collaborated in a BBC *Monitor* documentary based on his own life, and this began a new phase of activity, with many radio and TV plays, including *The Fall of Kelvin Walker* (1968).

Between 1972 and 1974 he was a member of a writers' group that also included Liz Lochhead and James Kelman. In 1981 his celebrated novel, *Lanark* was published, to immediate acclaim. From now on

Gray would concentrate on books, usually designed and illustrated, as well as written, by himself. *Unlikely Stories, Mostly* (1983) was followed by *1982, Janine* in 1984.

A retrospective exhibition of his work was shown in Glasgow, Edinburgh and Aberdeen in 1986. His first marriage had collapsed in 1969 and in 1991 he married Morag McAlpine. Many of Gray's murals have been destroyed through demolition and decay, but his original work can still be seen in the Abbot's House, Dunfermline, and at the Ubiquitous Chip restaurant in Glasgow. His designs can also be seen on the walls and ceilings of Glasgow's Oran Mor.

GREIG, SAMUEL
(1735–1788)
NAVAL COMMANDER

Samuel Greig was born in Inverkeithing in Fife. He joined the British navy initially, and was serving as a first mate, but in 1763 with the promise of promotion to a higher rank, he signed up for the Russian navy of Catherine the Great. He was to rise from Captain to Admiral within the next eighteen years.

Greig distinguished himself in the war against the Turks from 1768 to 1772 and was promoted for his efforts, first to Rear-Admiral in 1770 and then to vice-admiral in 1773. He was also responsible for the reconstruction of the port of Kronstadt, where he served as governor, and played a major role in the rebuilding of the flagging Russian navy into a formidable fighting force. When Russia entered into war with Sweden in 1788, Greig led the Russian fleet in the Baltic, once more with great distinction.

Greig received many honours for his work in Russia, including the Order of St George, the Order of St Anna, the Order of St Vladimir and the Order of St Andrew. His achievements were also noted in Great Britain and he became a Fellow of the Royal Society in 1781. He was still serving aboard ship when he fell ill and died in 1788 and he was given a state funeral in Russia.

GUTHRIE, JAMES
(1859–1930)
PAINTER

James Guthrie was born in Greenock. He studied law for a brief period at Glasgow University, but did not complete the course. His training as a painter was minimal, and although he did receive some guidance from John Pettie at the start of his career, he was largely self-taught. His early career brought him into contact with many of the young painters of the Glasgow School, 'The Glasgow Boys', and he is counted among the most prominent of their number. Collectively, the Glasgow Boys were much influenced by the work of the Hague School and of French painters of the latter part of the nineteenth century, such as Courbet, Corot and Bastien-Lepage. Their work moved away from the academic narrative style which had been dominating the taste of the artistic establishment of the time, towards greater realism both in choice and in treatment of subject. Individually, the Glasgow Boys came from diverse backgrounds and their work was to progress in different ways. Guthrie made the acquaintance of Joseph Crawhall (who came from the northeast of England) and EA Walton in 1878–79, when they made their first painting trip together to Rosneath. In 1880, they spent time together again, painting at Brig o' Turk. They painted from life, choosing their subjects from the people and landscapes they saw around them.

While some of the gathering group of young painters (which came to include George Henry, EA Hornel, John Lavery and others) attended winter classes in the studio of WY Macgregor in the coming years, Guthrie remained separate from them, but in the summer he would be among those who gathered at Cockburnspath in Berwickshire to paint. In 1882, Guthrie had completed a work that he had begun at Brig o' Turk, *A Highland Funeral*, generally considered to be his first major work. It was exhibited in 1883 at the Glasgow Institute and drew the attention of Arthur Melville, a more experienced painter whose own work was already progressing independently along the same lines as Guthrie's. Melville joined the painters at Cockburnspath and his work added to the melting pot of influences and ideas.

Guthrie was a pivotal figure in the group in its early days, which pooled resources and exchanged ideas with great enthusiasm. A growing confidence in handling paint, evident in the controlled fluidity of his brushwork, manifested itself in major works in the years following.

This confidence was allied with a more assuredly sympathetic treatment of subject. In later years, the painters of the Glasgow School diversified; Hornel and Henry's work, for example, became more decorative and symbolic. Guthrie moved into portraiture in his later years as a painter. In 1888, he became an Associate of the Royal Scottish Academy, and in 1902, its president. Notable paintings by Guthrie include *To Pastures New* (1883), *A Hind's Daughter* (1883), *Schoolmates* (1884), *In The Orchard* (1885), *The Reverend Andrew Gardiner* (1890), a portrait, and *Midsummer* (1892).

HAIG, DOUGLAS, 1ST EARL OF BEMERSYDE
(1861–1928)
MILITARY LEADER

Douglas Haig was born in Edinburgh and was educated in Edinburgh and Oxford before going to Sandhurst. He was in active service as a cavalry officer in Egypt and in the Boer War and served with distinction. He then served in India, rising to the position of Chief of Staff. He returned to England and took command of Aldershot and when war broke out in 1914, he went to France as Commander of the 1st Corps of the British Expeditionary Force. In 1915, he became Commander-in-Chief of the British Forces. In the next two years, Haig saw many thousands of his men die in an exhausting and relentless struggle against the German forces. He finally led the decisive offensive that led to the armistice in 1918, but was left with an enduring horror at the terrible cost of the war in terms of human life. He was made an earl in 1919 in honour of his achievements as a soldier, and after the war he dedicated himself to the welfare of ex-servicemen, the families of those who had fallen, and the wounded. In 1921, he became the first President of the newly founded British Legion.

Haig is buried at Dryburgh Abbey.

HARDIE, JAMES KEIR
(1856–1915)
Founder of the Scottish Labour Party

Keir Hardie was born on August 15th, 1856 in Legbrannock, Ayrshire. His father was a ship's carpenter. His working life began well before his childhood was over. At the age of seven, he had a job as an errand boy and at the age of ten, he started work down the coalmines. After twelve years down the pit, taking classes at night school in an effort to get himself a proper education, he lost his job at the pit at which he was working and was blacklisted by the mine owners for trying to organise the miners. He moved to Hamilton where he ran a newsagent's shop and also found work as a journalist. He still remained active in championing the cause of the working man and in particular the miners, helping set up organisations in Lanarkshire and Ayrshire, and in 1886, when the Scottish Miner's Federation was formed, Hardie became secretary. In 1888 Hardie became the founding chairman of the new Scottish Labour Party and stood for Mid-Lanark, but was defeated. Four years later, in 1892, he was successfully elected to parliament for West Ham South and in 1900 became MP for Merthyr Tydfil. He started two papers, *The Miner* and *The Labour Leader* in 1887 and 1889 respectively.

In 1893, The Independent Labour Party was formed, with Keir Hardie as leader. He remained in this post until 1900, and took the chair again in 1906 only to resign shortly afterwards due to ill health. In 1913 he became chairman once more. He was also chairman of the International Socialist Bureau in 1914, and in an attempt to prevent war, tried to organise trade unions in all countries involved into a general strike. His efforts failed, however and he was bitterly disappointed and disillusioned. He died in September, 1915.

HASTINGS, ANDREW GAVIN
(1962–)
RUGBY PLAYER

Born in Edinburgh, Gavin Hastings attended George Watson's College and went on to study land economy at Paisley College of Technology and Cambridge University. However, the basis of his life and career has been the game of rugby, at which he excelled from his schooldays. A Rugby Blue at Cambridge, he won his first cap for Scotland in 1986, playing against France, with his brother Scott also in the side. Gavin kicked six penalty goals and Scotland won 18–17. Hastings played for Scotland in three rugby World Cups, and altogether won 61 caps for his country, captaining the side on 20 occasions. Among the historic achievements in which he participated are the 1990 Grand Slam, and Scotland's first away victory in France for 26 years (1995). On retiring from the international game in that year, Hastings had scored over 700 points, making him second-highest test match point scorer after Australia's Michael Lynagh. Since 1995 Hastings has run his own sports marketing and sponsorship business, gives motivational talks to business groups, and has been a regular sports commentator and journalist.

HENDRY, STEPHEN
(1969–)
SNOOKER PLAYER

During the 1990s, Stephen Hendry won 28 ranking titles in snooker championships, among many other victories. Born in Auchterarder, Perthshire, he first showed his exceptional skill with a cue by winning the national under-16 championship in 1983; in the following year he became Scottish Amateur Champion. He turned professional aged only 16, and became the youngest ever Scottish professional champion, establishing himself rapidly as a contender for international success. By age 21 he was the world's top-ranked snooker player and the youngest-ever world champion. Hendry became the first player ever to make five centuries in seven frames, and is one of only five to win both the World and UK Championships in the same year. With Steve Davis and John Higgins he is one of three who held the World, UK and Masters titles at the same time. Hendry also holds the record for most centuries by one player in a tournament, with 16 centuries during the 2002 World Championship. Voted Player of the Year six times in the 1990s, Hendry was No. 1 on the ranking list for eight years. He made over 600 century breaks and has earned almost £8 million in prize money. In 1994 he was made MBE and has twice been voted BBC Scotland's Sports Personality of the Year.

HENRYSON, ROBERT
(*c.*1425–1508)
Poet

Associated with Dunfermline, Henryson is traditionally said to have been a schoolteacher, though he may have been a notary, or lawyer. Details of his personal life are scanty. Undoubtedly, though, he was a poet of great distinction, a leading member of the generation of poets once known as 'the Scots Chaucerians', who were inspired by Chaucer but who wrote in Scots and brought their own traditions and perspectives to bear. Henryson's major poem, 'The Testament of Cresseid', was often attached to Chaucer's *Troilus and Criseyde*. This was a self-consciously classic work, with a strong moral tone, which is also found in Henryson's versions of *Aesop's Fables*, along with humour and enchanting naturalistic detail.

Henryson's gift for comedy and psychological perception comes out most strongly in 'Robyne and Makyne', a story of failed love in which Robin is the first known portrayal of a certain kind of grim, repressed

Scot who realises too late that his false macho front has lost him everything he really wants.

HOGG, JAMES
(1770–1835)
Novelist and Poet

One of the most gifted and visionary writers in Scottish literature, Hogg was born in the Ettrick Forest and his schooling was punctuated by herding. His interest in poetry was sparked off in his teens, but he is not known to have written verse until he was in his 20s. An attempt to make his name with a pamphlet, *Scottish Pastorals, Poems, Songs, Etc.*, was a failure in 1801, and Hogg considered moving to the Isle of Harris. Things looked up in 1803 when he sent some samples of his work to Walter Scott, who included them in Vol. 3 of *Minstrelsy of the Scottish Border* and became a friend. Rather like Burns, Hogg found literature not to be financially rewarding, and had to fall back on rather unsuccessful farming. Nevertheless he became a familiar figure in Edinburgh literary society. He married Margaret Phillips, a farmer's daughter, in 1820, but she kept his house while he visited Edinburgh friends and, on one occasion, London. In 1824 he published *The Private Memoirs and Confessions of a Justified Sinner*, a highly original novel which probes deep into Calvinistic morality and the Scottish fascination with the dual personality: its reputation increases as time goes on. Hogg's reputation was clouded by the clownish persona of 'The Ettrick Shepherd' wished upon him by 'Christopher North'

(John Wilson) in the essays in *Blackwood's Magazine* which supposedly described their convivial evenings in Ambrose's Tavern in Edinburgh. In fact Wilson was the buffoon. If Hogg had written only the beautiful lyric *Kilmeny* and *The Confessions of a Justified Sinner* he would have a respected place in English literature, but his output was much wider and, though uneven, well repays reading.

HOLLOWAY, RICHARD
(1933–)
THEOLOGIAN AND ETHICAL THINKER

Until 2000 'Primus', or senior bishop, of the Episcopal Church in Scotland, in that role Holloway had already expressed many controversial views and since becoming what one newspaper called 'a public intellectual', his participation in topical discussion has increased. Born in Glasgow in 1933, he grew up in Alexandria, Dunbartonshire, and trained for the Anglican priesthood at Kelham Theological College, Edinburgh Theological College, and Union Theological Seminary, New York. He met his wife, Jean, in America, and they have three children. Holloway was Professor of Divinity at Gresham College, London, before being appointed Bishop of Edinburgh in 1986. He became Primus in 1992. But his personal journey has been away from orthodox and organised religion towards something closer to humanism. As his book (one of many) *Godless Morality* (1999) suggests, he believes that we should look within ourselves and our society for guidance on ethical questions. He has campaigned on behalf of gay rights, and many other liberal causes. Much in demand as a broadcaster and public speaker, he is chair of the Scottish Arts Council.

HOY, SIR CHRISTOPHER (CHRIS)
(1976–)
Olympic Sportsman

Edinburgh-born Chris Hoy is Scotland's most successful Olympic athlete, winner of three gold medals at the Beijing Olympics in 2008, the first Briton to achieve this for 100 years. A former pupil of George Watson's College, he attended St Andrews University, then Moray House College of Education where he graduated in sports science in 1999. Seeing the film *ET* at the age of six inspired him to cycle and he became a highly successful boy racer on BMX bikes. In 1992 he joined cycling club Dunedin CC and from 1994 concentrated on track cycling with the City of Edinburgh Racing Club. Between then and 2008 his career progressed from the simple 'Kilo' time trial race over one kilometre to the more complex and tactical 'Keirin' race where judgement as well as power is essential. The Kilo gave him his first world title in 2002 and the Olympic gold in 2004. In the 2008 Olympics he won gold in the Men's Keirin, the Men's Team Sprint, and the Men's Individual Sprint. His exceptional achievement has won him other laurels, including a knighthood and the title of Sportsman of the Year and Sports Personality of the Year in 2008. The National Velodrome being built for the 2014 Commonweath Games in Glasgow will bear his name.

HUME, DAVID
(1711–1776)
Philosopher

David Hume was born in Edinburgh. He studied law at Edinburgh University for a period but abandoned his studies in order to write. He travelled to France, and living in Anjou for three years, he wrote his first major work, *A Treatise of Human Nature*, published anonymously in 1739. To his great disappointment, the book (which was many years later recognised as a masterpiece), was received with little enthusiasm. Hume stayed at the family home in Ninewells, Berwickshire from 1739 to 1745 and during this period published *Essays Moral and Political*, which were considerably more successful than *Treatise*. He applied for the post of professor of Moral Philosophy at Edinburgh University in 1744, but failed to secure the post because of his atheism.

In 1745, Hume left home to tutor the Marquis of Annandale, who was insane, and in 1746 travelled to France as the secretary of General St Clair. On his return to Scotland in 1748, he worked on a revised and simplified version of the Treatise and published it under the title of *An Enquiry Concerning Human Understanding*. It was only a little more successful than Treatise had been, but it drew the attention of some of the great thinkers in Europe at the time. His next work, *Political*

Discourses, brought him recognition and acclaim and was a considerable influence on ADAM SMITH, author of *The Wealth of Nations 1776*, with whom he became friends. Hume had written another work at this time, *Dialogues Concerning Natural Religion*, but quite prudently left it unpublished as its content was too controversial. It was eventually published after his death.

In 1751, Hume applied for the chair of Logic at Glasgow University, but once more, he was unsuccessful. He was appointed keeper of the Advocate's Library in Edinburgh in 1752 and during this period, produced another major work, the five-volume *History of England*, which was very well received, and also *Four Dissertations*.

From 1763 to 1766, Hume worked in France as Secretary to the British Embassy in Paris and found literary society there much more receptive to his ideas. He made the acquaintance of Rousseau and returned with him to England, where he worked as secretary to General Conway for the next two years. In 1769, he returned to Edinburgh, where he spent the last years of his life in the company of intellectual friends and acquaintances, including Adam Smith. He died peacefully after a long illness in 1776.

HUNTER, SIR THOMAS BLANE (TOM)
(1961–)
BUSINESSMAN

Though the recession of 2008–9 has trimmed the scale

of his wealth and giving, Hunter is reckoned to be Scotland's first home-grown billionaire, with a fortune, in 2007, of £1.05 billion. He was born in New Cumnock and attended Cumnock Academy, then Strathclyde University Business School. In classic fashion his career took off from selling goods from the back of a van; in his case it was trainers, just at the time when such footwear was becoming fashionable. In 1989 he opened his first Sports Division store, in Paisley. From this it grew into the UK's largest chain of sportswear shops, until Hunter sold it to JJB Sports in 1998. Since then, he has concentrated on property development and business investment and during the expansive years up to 2008 his investments made him very rich. Inspired by Andrew Carnegie's dictum, 'He who dies rich, dies disgraced', he and his wife established the Hunter Foundation in 1998 as a means of supporting charitable, educational and entrepreneurial projects in Scotland and elsewhere. He received a knighthood in 2005 for 'services to philanthropy and entrepreneurship in Scotland'.

INGLIS, ELSIE MAUD
(1864–1917)
PIONEER IN WOMEN'S MEDICINE

Elsie Inglis was born in Naini Tal in India. When she was twenty-two years old, she came to Scotland to begin her studies in Edinburgh at the new School of Medicine for Women. From there she went to continue her studies in Glasgow under the tuition of the eminent surgeon Sir William McEwen. She went to London after she became qualified in 1892 and it was here, working in a general hospital in the capital, that she became dedicated to the cause of women's suffrage and also to the campaign for specialised medical care for women, given by women.

She returned to Edinburgh two years later and started her own practice with another woman doctor. She expanded her horizons by opening a maternity hospital in 1904, in the High Street; a hospital for women, run by women. The Elsie Inglis Memorial Hospital as it became known in later years did much to increase the standards of care provided for the women of the city and in particular, for the poor. Her belief in the need for women's suffrage never faltered and she became the founder of the Scottish Women's Suffragette Federation in 1906.

A tireless and dedicated doctor, Elsie Inglis took a courageous and innovative role in the first World War. Sidestepping the red tape which prevented her from giving her services to the military or the Red Cross, she found independent funding to equip and staff mobile medical units for France and Serbia. She herself went to Serbia and there set up three hospitals, all run by women, which did extremely valuable work in the battle against the spread of the rampant infections such as typhoid that were such merciless killers at that time. She was taken prisoner and repatriated in 1916, but, undaunted, she promptly set about raising money to go to Russia to set up and run another hospital. She was forced finally to return to Britain in the autumn of the next year, as she was suffering from cancer and was too ill to continue her work. She died some weeks later.

JAMES VI AND I
(1566–1625)
KING OF SCOTLAND AND ENGLAND

James, the son of Mary, Queen of Scots and Lord Darnley, was born in Edinburgh Castle. Following the enforced abdication of Mary, James became king when he was little more than a year old and a succession of regents held power on his behalf. The Earl of Moray, the first regent, was murdered in 1570, and Lennox, the second was killed in 1571. The Earl of Mar succeeded Lennox but died in 1572, when James Douglas, Earl of Morton became regent.

In spite of an attempt by the Earls of Atholl and Argyll to seize power in 1782, the Earl of Morton lasted until 1581, when he was executed at the instigation of The Duke of Lennox and the Earl of Arran. James was taken captive in revenge and held at Ruthven Castle, a move which won the approval of the General Assembly. He escaped and in the coming months, the authority of the crown was firmly reasserted and rebel Presbyterians were forced to flee. James believed in the Divine Right of Kings and in his determination to enforce his authority as supreme, was continually at odds with the Church and the nobility of Scotland. However, his efforts to subdue his nobles were rewarded and his struggles against the extremes of Catholic and Protestant faiths succeeded in producing a degree of stability.

When his mother faced execution in 1587, James protested, but did not intervene on her behalf, preferring to avoid conflict with Elizabeth I. In 1589, he married Anne of Denmark. His return from Denmark was delayed by a storm, believed by the king to have been raised by witches, and he took care to supervise the torture and death of those accused, in the trials at North Berwick in 1591. This cruel streak manifested itself again soon after James succeeded to the throne of England in 1603. In 1605, he took a personal interest in the torture of Guy Fawkes following the Gunpowder Plot.

James spent more time in England than in Scotland in the following years, preferring to rule the Scots from a distance. His popularity in England waned considerably as he warred with parliament, forced conformity to the Anglican Church upon the Puritans, and kept his 'favourites', such as Robert Carr and George Villiers (preferred for their looks rather than their political wisdom) in prominence in his court. His international policy was one of peace and he made every effort to keep England from war. This resulted in a decline in England's status as a naval power and a loss of influence overseas. His efforts to keep peace with Spain in particular were not well received by people or parliament.

In spite of his unpopularity with many of his subjects, James is judged to have been one of the most successful rulers of Scotland, bringing greater stability to the country and assisting the progress of industry. As an intellectual, he contributed to his country's culture in no small way when he commissioned a new translation of the Bible, known as the King James Version.

James was succeeded by his younger son, Charles I in 1625.

JONES, JOHN PAUL (ORIGINAL NAME JOHN PAUL)
(1747–1792)
AMERICAN NAVAL COMMANDER

John Paul was born in Kirkcudbright and went to sea as a cabin boy when he was still young, sailing on a ship to America. He continued his sailing career in slave ships where he progressed through the ranks and became notorious for his cruel discipline, narrowly avoiding a conviction for manslaughter following the death of a crewman whom he had flogged. In 1773, he escaped from another similar charge following the mutiny of his crew in the West Indies, and now an outlaw in the eyes of the British, settled in Friedericksburg and changed his name to John Paul Jones. When the American Revolution broke out he joined the navy, sailing as a lieutenant on the American ship *Alfred*. He was promoted to the rank of captain in 1776 and in command of the vessel *Ranger* sailed to Scotland and the Solway Firth, causing considerable damage to British ships.

Promoted once again, this time to the rank of

commodore and sailing from France, Jones took command of the *Bonhomme Richard* and set out with a fleet of five French vessels to British waters once again. In a great battle against British ships in 1779, his ship was victorious against the man o' war *Serapis*. He returned to the United States and prepared to take command of the magnificent vessel *America* in 1781, but he was finally deprived of the chance to sail in her and was returned to service in Europe. In recognition of his efforts in the war against the British, he was awarded a gold medal of Congress – the only naval officer to have received this honour.

In 1788, Jones entered the Russian navy and fought in the Russo-Turkish war as commander of the Black Sea squadron until 1789. He then retired to France, where he died in 1792.

KELMAN, JAMES
(1946–)
NOVELIST, PLAYWRIGHT

James Kelman was born and brought up in Glasgow. He served two years of an apprenticeship as a compositor, then moved with his family to America for a short time. He found work only sporadically and was unemployed for a considerable amount of time. His ambitions to write for a living began to be fulfilled with the popular reception given to publication of his first book of short stories: *Not Not While the Giro* in 1983. His reputation grew with the publication of three more books in the next four years: *The Busconductor Hines* (1984), *A Chancer*

(1985), and *Greyhound for Breakfast* (1987). He won the Cheltenham Prize for *Greyhound for Breakfast* and *A Disaffection*, published two years later, won the James Tait Black Memorial Prize and was shortlisted for the Booker Prize. A book of three plays, *Hardie and Baird and other Plays*, was published in 1991 and *The Burn* was published in 1992. Kelman's most notable achievement is the Booker Prize which he won in 1994 for *How Late it Was, How Late*. His own (often relentlessly grim) brand of social realism and his unsentimental portrayal of poverty and related social problems reflect his own moral and political concerns and have influenced many contemporary Scottish writers, although critics of his work frequently fix on the extensive use of offensive language in his books.

Kelman spent three semesters teaching at the University of Texas and has also been associated with Goldsmiths College, London and the University of Glasgow. He lives in Glasgow with his wife and family and is still writing. In 1999, a series of short stories, *The Good Times*, was published, and won the Stakis Prize for Scottish Writer of the Year (shared with Edwin Morgan). In 2008 he won the Saltire Society's Book of the Year Award for *Kieron Smith, boy* (2008).

KENNEDY, ALISON LOUISE (AL)
(1965–)

Writer

In typically self-deprecatory style, AL Kennedy has written that 'someone who sits alone typing for hours at a time must be really fascinating'. Born in Dundee, she now lives in Glasgow. A performer as well as a writer, Kennedy occasionally does stand-up comedy. She has taught creative writing at St Andrews and Warwick Universities and has been on the judging panel of the Orange Prize for Fiction and other prizes.

She has won many prizes herself, including the Saltire Best First Book Award for *Night Geometry and the Garscadden Trains* (1990) and the Somerset Maugham Award for *Looking for the Possible Dance* (1993). Her books have been translated into several European languages and she was awarded the Austrian State Prize for Literature in 2008.

There is a wry, stoical, often dark element in Kennedy's observation and humour, perhaps related to her own experience of physical pain from spinal problems, as well as to life in general.

KENNETH I (MAC-ALPIN)
(*c*. 800–858)
King of Scots, *c.*840–858;
King of Picts, *c.* 843–858

Kenneth was the son of Alpin, the 34th king of the Dalriadan Scots. His ascent to kingship over the Picts was most likely to have been achieved partly through hereditary claim through maternal descent, and partly with the use of force. Scandinavian attacks had been wreaking havoc among the Picts and as a result their strength was considerably diminished, a circumstance which Kenneth could exploit in his favour. According to one tale of his conquests, he invited rulers of leading Pictish families to dine with him and, having dug a concealed pit behind the benches upon which his guests sat, he contrived to have them tipped backwards into the pit and slaughtered. By 846, all Pictish resistance to his rule had been effectively subdued. As the Dalriadan Scots migrated into the lands of the Picts and as continual raids from the Vikings threatened the coast, Kenneth moved the centre of his kingdom eastwards, possibly to Forteviot. He moved the relics of St Columba from Iona to Dunkeld in 849, either enlarging an existing religious centre or establishing a new one. He was also responsible for establishing Scone as a religious centre and the place where the kings of Alba would be crowned, and there have been suggestions that it was he who first brought the Stone of Destiny there.

The reign of Kenneth I was a turbulent one. His people were subject to frequent raids from the Vikings, Danes and Britons during that period and whilst employing considerable resources in repelling these attacks, Kenneth also sought to extend his power southwards, making several incursions into Lothian and into Saxon territory.

Kenneth died in 858, as a result of illness.

KING, JESSIE MARION
(1875–1949)
PAINTER AND ILLUSTRATOR

Jessie M King was born in New Kilpatrick, where her

father was parish minister. Despite his initial opposition she trained as an artist, first at Queen Margaret College, then at the Glasgow School of Art, from 1892. In 1899 she became tutor in book decoration and design there – at a time when book design was a highly esteemed craft, and when the 'Glasgow Style', related to *Art Nouveau,* was being fully developed. From about 1905 she also designed fabrics and jewellery, with solo shows in London (1905) and Glasgow (1907). She was also a member of the Glasgow Society of Lady Artists. After a ten-year engagement, she married the craftsman-artist Ernest Archibald Taylor in 1908 and they lived in Salford, where their only child, Merle Elspeth, was born in 1909, before moving in 1910 to Paris. King continued with illustration, exhibiting at the Salon and the 1914 *Arts Décoratifs* exhibition. Each summer, they ran painting courses at High Corrie, Isle of Arran, and applied arts courses in the artists' colony of Kirkcudbright, where they settled in 1915. Wearing wide-brimmed hats and buckled shoes like a nursery-rhyme character, King (known as Jake) became a notable figure in Kirkcudbright, where she organized and designed community pageants. She was cremated there and her ashes were scattered at the church of Minard, Argyll. In the 1940s and 50s, her work was not highly regarded, but from the 1970s, her idiosyncratic art has steadily risen in critical and commercial favour.

KENTIGERN, SAINT (ALSO KNOWN AS SAINT MUNGO)

(*c.*520–*c.*614)

PATRON SAINT OF GLASGOW

Little is known about the life of St Kentigern that can be established as fact. Accounts of the manner of his conception and nature of his birth vary, as do details of the events in his life. He is said to have been the illegitimate son of Princess Thenew of Lothian. When Thenew's pregnancy was discovered, she was cast adrift in a boat in the Firth of Forth and was washed up on the coast of Fife at Culross, where her son was born. He was named Kentigern and was educated at Culross by St Serf in his monastery. Kentigern was given the name Mungo (meaning 'dear friend') as an affectionate nickname. From Culross, he went to a place called Kernach where he met an old man called Fergus. Fergus died while with Kentigern, and Kentigern took the old man's body to Crathures, later called Glasgow, where he buried it in a cemetery consecrated by St Ninian. He stayed there for some years, founded a monastery and was consecrated as a bishop. When he left Glasgow *c.*553 after a dispute with King Morken, he went to Wales where he founded a monastery and was said to have met St David and St Asaph. He returned to Strathclyde, and various stories of miracles are associated with his life during this period. He met St Columba who came to see him at the Molindar, where he lived.

St Kentigern died *c.*614 and was buried on the site of Glasgow Cathedral, which is named St Mungo's Cathedral after him. He is the patron saint of Glasgow, and is also acknowledged as founder of the city.

KERR, DEBORAH
(1921–2007)
ACTRESS

Deborah Jane Kerr-Trimmer was born in Helensburgh. She trained in England as a ballet dancer and became a member of the corps-de-ballet with the Sadler's Wells company in the late 1930s, but she chose to change the course of her career soon afterwards and to take up acting as a profession. She began working as an actress in repertory theatre but it was not long before she moved into the world of film. Her first film appearances were in the 1940s, in British movies which included *Major Barbara* (1940), *Courageous Mr Penn* (1941), *The Life and Death of Colonel Blimp* (1943) and *Black Narcissus* (1947). She then moved to Hollywood where she had been offered a contract, and several more films followed. Her appearance as an emotionally troubled adultress in the classic movie *From Here to Eternity* in 1953 was a departure from the more ladylike roles to which her audience had become accustomed to her playing, but it was nonetheless a critical success and won her a nomination for an Academy Award. She also enjoyed box-office success with her starring roles in *The King and I* (1956) and *An Affair to Remember* (1957). With five other Academy Award nominations to her credit,

Deborah Kerr stepped back from the big screen in 1969, but continued to work regularly and successfully on the stage and in television drama in the following years. She returned to the world of film in 1985 to appear in *The Assam Garden*. In 1993, she was given an honorary Academy Award for Lifetime Achievement, and in 1998 awarded a CBE.

She died of Parkinson's disease in 2007 at the age of 86.

KIDD, WILLIAM
(*c.*1645–1701)
PIRATE

William Kidd was born in Greenock. Little is known of his early years but he is thought to have taken to the seafaring life as a young man. By 1690, he had become well-established as the owner of several ships sailing out of New York. In 1695 he travelled to England and was given a commission as a privateer, battling against the pirates that were posing a threat to the trading ships in the Indian Ocean. He sailed for Madagascar in the ship *Adventure*, but when he reached there it appeared that he had turned to piracy himself, and several merchant ships, including the *Quedagh Merchant*, were attacked between 1697 and 1698, apparently at his instigation. He was declared a pirate and a warrant was put out for his capture. Kidd returned to the West Indies in 1699 to find that he was a wanted man. He proceeded to Boston where he gave himself over to the authorities voluntarily, believing that he would be able to justify his actions and secure a pardon. No pardon was forthcoming however, and Kidd was taken prisoner and sent back to England where he was tried and convicted of piracy. He was hanged for his crimes in May, 1701.

KNOX, JOHN
(1513–1572)
Leader of the Scottish Reformation

John Knox was born in Haddington. He is thought to have been educated at St Andrews University. He was ordained as a Catholic priest, but, influenced by the teachings of George Wishart in the 1550s, he turned to the Protestant ministry. When Wishart was executed by Cardinal Beaton in St Andrews 1546 and Protestant reformers killed Beaton in retaliation, Knox joined those who occupied St Andrews Castle and preached to them there. When the troops of Mary of Guise captured the castle, Knox was taken prisoner and spent eighteen months in the galleys. Edward VI interceded on his behalf, and when Knox was released he went to England where his stance against the practices of the Catholic church found greater sympathy. He was appointed a royal chaplain, but when Mary Tudor, a Roman Catholic, came to the throne, he fled to Geneva, where he became acquainted with Protestant reformer John Calvin. Knox remained in Geneva until 1559, visiting Scotland to preach once during this period. In 1558, his treatise *The First Blast of the Trumpet Against the Monstrous Regiment of Women* was published, aimed against Mary Tudor and Mary of Guise. He returned to Scotland in 1559 and his preaching at Perth, St Andrews and Edinburgh won him strong support. The Protestant reformers rose in revolt against the Catholic regent and were granted military support from England. They were helped to success when Mary of Guise died and the French troops supporting her were withdrawn. The Protestants took control. *A Confession of Faith* was written and adopted, establishing Protestantism as the authorised creed, and Knox was one of six ministers who drew up *The First Book of Discipline*, outlining the organisation of the church. When MARY QUEEN OF SCOTS returned to Scotland in 1561, she found a Protestant-led government ruling the country and the Church of Scotland well-established with Knox as minister at St Giles.

Knox made no secret of his antagonism towards Mary. He loudly condemned her for holding mass at her court and argued with her on several occasions in person. Whilst she was for compromise, Knox would not contemplate it. Knox supported the murder of Rizzio, but took no part in it; nor did he play any part in enforcing the abdication of Mary after the murder of Darnley, although he preached at the coronation of the infant JAMES VI. He withdrew from the troubles after Rizzio's death and went to Ayrshire, where he wrote the *History of the Reformation in Scotland*.

In 1572, Knox moved to St Andrews. By now he was severely disabled after a stroke. He returned to preach his last sermon at St Giles in November 1572 and died later that month.

LAUDER, SIR HARRY
(1870–1950)
MUSIC HALL ENTERTAINER

Harry Lauder was born in Portobello. The son of a potter, he worked from boyhood, first in a flax mill and then in the mines, before winning a singing contest and making the decision to try to earn a living on the stage. He embarked upon his career in the music halls as a comedian, but his songs were to gain him greater popularity. Many of them, such as 'Roamin' in the Gloamin', and 'I Love a Lassie', both of which he composed himself, became favourites of the age and are remembered with great affection today. His fame spread across the border and his 'cheeky chappie' manner, his glengarry, kilt and twisted walking stick became well-beloved by the English as much as the Scots. From England, Lauder moved on to tour in the United States where, once more, his concerts were a resounding success. His performances were not sophisticated: they were, quite simply, entertaining.

During World War I, Harry Lauder organised entertainment for the troops. The war brought him personal tragedy when his son was killed in action and this inspired him to write another timeless favourite; 'Keep Right on to the End of the Road', which is remembered as a community song of both World Wars.

When Lauder died in 1950, he left behind a legacy of singalong classics and for those who had seen him perform, a memory of fine times at the concert hall.

LAW, DENIS

(1940–)

FOOTBALLER

Denis Law was born in Aberdeen on February 24, 1940. He crossed the border from his homeland into England to begin his professional career and made his debut with Huddersfield Town in 1956. He stayed with Huddersfield until 1959 when he joined the team at Manchester City before being transferred to Torino in Italy in 1961. The talent of the young Torino player was noticed by Matt Busby and in 1962, Denis was bought for Manchester United for a record-breaking transfer fee.

It is with Manchester United and Old Trafford that Law's name will always be associated. The team enjoyed a series of successes during Law's years with them as a player and the successes owed much to the player's legendary skills as a footballer. His goal-scoring ability was hard to beat, and indeed, as a player for Scotland, his record of 30 goals was equalled only by KENNY DALGLISH. His years with Manchester United saw him play with them as a winning side in the League Championship in 1964–65 and 1966–67 and in the FA Cup in 1962–63. Sadly, however, he was prevented from sharing in their momentous European Cup victory in 1968, because of a knee injury.

He was capped a total of fifty-five times for Scotland.

The knee injury which had affected him during 1968 still caused Law problems. He was transferred to Manchester City in 1973, and there he remained till the end of his playing career. Law will always be a player to remember. He is recognised as one of the wizards of the game. His interest and involvement in football continues with participation in television and radio commentaries and discussions, and guest appearances at sports-related functions.

LENNOX, ANN (ANNIE)
(1954–)
SINGER AND SONG-WRITER

Born in Aberdeen on Christmas Day, Annie Lennox is an only child of working-class parents, who encouraged her talents. After Aberdeen High School for Girls, she won a place at the Royal Academy of Music in London. Classical music was not to be her career, though, and after three difficult years in London, in 1977–80 she became lead singer of The Tourists pop band. Also involved was Dave Stewart who collaborated with her in the synth-pop duo The Eurythmics, which had a highly successful run right through the 80s. From 1990, Lennox embarked on a solo career, making astute and successful use of video in promotion and performance, with a series of hit albums, including *Diva* (1992), *Bare* (2003) and *Songs of Mass Destruction* (2007). As her themes often suggest, Lennox has always been an artist with a strong social conscience, working for Shelter and African AIDS charities among others.

In 1984 she married Radha Raman but it lasted for less than a year. In 1988 she married Uri Fruchtmann and they had two daughters. The marriage ended in 2000.

LIDDELL, ERIC HENRY
(1902–1945)
ATHLETE, MISSIONARY

Eric Liddell, the son of two missionaries, was born in Tientsin in China. He attended Eltham College in England and went on to study at Edinburgh University. Liddell had a remarkable gift for running and was capable of producing sprinting speeds that far outstripped the capabilities of many of his peers. His speed stood him in great stead in his other sport, rugby, and he played wing three-quarters for Scotland seven times. Liddell was a committed sportsman, but he was more committed to his Christian faith, and in 1924, as part of the British Olympic Squad in Paris, he forfeited what would have almost certainly have been a gold medal in the 100 metres because the heats for the event were scheduled to be run on a Sunday, a day which he believed should be sacred. Harold Abrahams, his team mate, won the event in his place. Liddell ran in the 200 metres and won a bronze medal, and then went on to win a gold medal in the 400 metres, a race in which he was much less practised, breaking the world record as he did so.

In 1925, he went to China to work as a missionary for the Scottish Congregational Church. In 1934 he married Florence Mackenzie but they were separated by the war when his family moved to Canada for safety.

He was interned by the Japanese in World War II and he died in internment at Weifeng in February 1945. An Oscar-winning film of Liddell's and Abraham's Olympic story, *Chariots of Fire*, was made in 1981. Liddell is remembered for his work as a missionary at Weifeng, where a statue has been built in his honour, and also in the city of Edinburgh, where a church-run community centre bears his name.

LIVINGSTONE, DR DAVID
(1813–1873)
MISSIONARY, EXPLORER

David Livingstone was born in Blantyre. He was sent to work in a cotton mill at the age of ten, but he continued to study independently and at the age of twenty four, he left the mill to study medicine in Glasgow with the intention of becoming a medical missionary. He also studied theology and was ordained by the London Missionary Society. He was posted, in 1841, to South Africa where he worked in Bechauanaland, in a settlement run by Robert Moffat. In 1845, Livingstone married Moffat's daughter Mary. In spite of active opposition from the Boers, the Livingstones travelled northward and visited areas until then never seen by any other European. They crossed the Kalahari desert and discovered Lake Mgami in 1849. In 1852–1856, in an attempt to open up trade routes from east and west to the interior, Livingstone found the Victoria

Falls on the Zambesi. He returned to Britain in 1856 and published an account of his exploits in *Missionary Travels*. He resigned as a missionary and was appointed in 1858 by the British government as head of another expedition. The expedition explored the Zambesi and its tributaries further, and discovered Lake Nyasa. In 1862, Livingstone's wife Mary died at Shupunga. In 1863, the expedition was recalled and Livingstone returned to Britain independently via Bombay. In the book published after this expedition, *The Zambesi and its Tributaries*, Livingstone exposed the horrors of the slave trade which he had encountered during his travels.

Livingstone sailed for Africa once more in 1866, to discover the source of the Nile and study the rivers of East Central Africa. He explored the Ruvuma river, became the first European to see Lakes Mweru and Bangweulu, and reached Lake Tanganyika in failing health. He tried to continue his explorations with limited success, and concern mounted for him back in Britain. A party led by Henry Morton Stanley finally tracked Livingstone down in 1871 and the famous greeting, 'Dr Livingstone, I presume?' was uttered when the two met. Stanley accompanied Livingstone on an exploration north of the lake before Livingstone set off once more on his search for the source of the Nile. His health did not hold out and he died at Chitambo. His body was embalmed and returned to England for burial in Westminster Abbey.

LOCHHEAD, LIZ
(1947–)
POET, PLAYWRIGHT AND PERFORMER

Liz Lochhead was born in Motherwell in Lanarkshire. When she left school, she went to study painting at Glasgow School of Art, and after graduation went into teaching. In 1978, she was selected for the Scottish Canadian Writers' Exchange Fellowship and took up writing as a full-time career from that point. In the years since then her reputation as a playwright, poet and performer has steadily grown. Plays written by Lochhead include *Blood and Ice* (1982), *Disgusting Objects* (1982), *Sweet Nothings* (1984), *Shangahai'd*, *Rosaleen's Baby* and *Dracula*. In 1985, she was asked by the Lyceum Theatre Company to write a new translation of Molière's *Tartuffe*, the result of which, written in rhyming couplets in her own brand of 'theatrical Scots', as Lochhead called it, earned critical acclaim. In 1987, *Mary Queen of Scots Got Her Head Chopped Off* followed the success of *Tartuffe*. Lochhead also wrote the text for the musical production *Jock Tamson's Bairns*, which appeared in Glasgow in 1990. *Miseryguts* (2001) based on Molière's *Misanthrope*, also written in Scots, is set in the Scottish parliament.

Lochhead's poetry – witty, honest and direct – has proved equally popular and two of her collections of verse, *Dreaming Frankenstein and Collected Poems* and *True Confessions and New Clichés*, published in 1984 and 1985 respectively, have sold consistently well. In 1986, Lochhead was writer-in-residence at Edinburgh University, and writer-in-residence at the Royal Shakespeare Company in 1988. Lochhead has also written for television. She has given readings and performances of her work all over Britain. Edinburgh University awarded her an honorary degree in 2002. She lives in Glasgow.

LULU (MARIE MCDONALD MCLAUGHLAN LAWRIE)
(1948–)
POPULAR SINGER AND TELEVISION PERSONALITY

Marie McDonald Lawrie was born in Glasgow on November 3 1948. A diminutive figure with a big personality and a powerful voice, she stormed into the pop charts in 1964 with her first hit, a version of the Isley Brothers' 'Shout'. This record looked as if it might be a one-off success when six out of her eight following singles failed to get chart placings.

Then in 1966 she played a leading role in the film *To Sir with Love*, starring opposite Sydney Poitier. The film and the title song, which she recorded, were both commercial successes. In 1967, she had another hit with 'The Boat that I Row'. A string of British hits then followed, including 'Me, the Peaceful Heart' and 'I'm a Tiger' and she was offered her own series on television in the 1970s in which she proved her abilities as an entertainer and television personality. Lulu also took joint first place in the 1969 Eurovision Song Contest with 'Boom Bang-a-Bang'.

In the same year, she married Maurice, one of the Gibb brothers, better known as the Bee Gees. The marriage was a short-lived one, ending in 1973. In 1974 she sang the theme tune to the Bond film *The Man with the Golden Gun*.

Lulu has also acted in television, notably in *The Growing Pains of Adrian Mole* in 1987, in which she played the role of Adrian's mother. She showed that she doesn't take herself too seriously when she appeared as herself in several episodes of *French and Saunders* and also *Absolutely Fabulous*. In 1999 she appeared with Tom Courtenay in the British film *Whatever Happened to Harold Smith*.

As a singer Lulu has an enduring quality and still records and performs regularly. Collaboration with David Bowie in the 1980s brought her commercial success with 'The Man Who Sold the World'. In the 1990s she had a major hit with Independence and shared a hit with boy band Take That when they recorded 'Relight my Fire' together.

The beginning of the new millennium saw Lulu co-hosting and performing on the short-lived *Red Alert* National Lottery show on BBC television. In 2009, Lulu participated in the advertising campaign for Homecoming Scotland, a year-long campaign to encourage people from all around the world with Scottish heritage to visit Scotland. In January 2009, Lulu began a four-week stint as a coach on the BBC show *Eurovision: Your Country Needs You*, helping to choose the singer to represent the UK in the 2009 Eurovision song contest.

Lulu was awarded the OBE in the Queen's Birthday Honours 2000.

LYNCH, BENJAMIN JOHN (BENNY)
(1913–1946)
Boxer

Benny Lynch was born in the Gorbals in Glasgow, the second son of John Lynch, a railway worker of Irish descent, and his wife Lizzie. His mother left home shortly after the war and he and his brother James went to live with their uncle's family. They both started boxing at a local church boy's club. James looked set for a promising career as a boxer, but he died from meningitis. Benny abandoned amateur boxing shortly after that and ran wild for a period, getting involved in gang-fights in the streets around his home. Then he decided to return to boxing as a professional. He began training with Sammy Wilson, who took him under his wing and started him out on the road to featherweight championship. Under Wilson's guidance, Lynch won several minor bouts in permanent rings, and gained further experience in the fairground booths. His reputation grew rapidly. When he defeated the Italian champion, Carlo Cavagnoli, he became a hero. Sammy Wilson began to arrange fights through George Dingley, the promoter, and shortly after that, Lynch took the Scottish featherweight title from Jim Campbell. A rematch only resulted in a more convincing victory for Lynch. He continued with a punishing schedule of fights, the devastating force of his punching proving his prowess repeatedly. The fights brought him a sense of achievement, and money to spend on drinking and dancing.

In 1935, he married Annie McGuckian, but the marriage had difficulties and within four months they separated. Lynch had beaten champions from Britain and Europe, but there were signs that his drinking was becoming a problem. Later that year, Lynch became the first Scot to win the title of World Champion, beating Jackie Brown of America. He was reconciled with his wife for a brief period, but tensions with Wilson lead to him dismissing him as manager. His training became sporadic, interspersed with bouts of hard drinking. He suffered a crushing defeat at the hands of Jim Warnock, but won several fights in succession after that. A severe beating from Len Hampston was avenged in a later fight, which Lynch won. But it became harder to keep his weight down for fights and to get fit. He was an alcoholic, and his reputation was in rapid decline. In 1938, he lost his world title when he could not make fighting weight against Jackie Jurich. He also lost the support of Dingley.

After a fight against Aurel Toma, in which Lynch suffered a humiliating defeat and the first knockout of his career, he was taken to the monks at Mount Melleray to dry out, a last ditch effort that was unsuccessful. In 1939, his boxing licence was revoked. His marriage disintegrated. In 1946, he was admitted to hospital in a pitiful condition and died shortly afterwards.

McADAM, JOHN LOUDON
(1756–1836)
Road engineer

John McAdam was born in Ayr but emigrated to New York in 1770 where he went to work for his uncle in his counting-house. He remained in America for thirteen years, during which time he amassed a considerable fortune. He returned to Scotland and settled at Sauchrie, where he pursued his interests in engineering and privately began working on his theories for improving methods of road construction, funding his work himself. He was able to put his ideas into practice after 1816, when he was appointed surveyor to the Bristol Turnpike Trust. McAdam's roads were constructed by laying down a thick layer of broken stones, followed by a further quantity of smaller stones, or gravel. The smaller stones, impacted around and in between the larger ones, held the larger ones together and levelled the road to an almost smooth surface. In addition to this, McAdam raised the level of the road, giving it a camber to improve drainage. McAdam earned much acclaim for his work, although financially, it cost him dearly. He was consulted on several other road-building projects and finally, in 1827, he was made Surveyor-General of Metropolitan Roads. The term 'macadamised' is used to describe any road which has been constructed according to the principles devised by McAdam.

MACBETH
(1005–1057)
KING OF SCOTS, 1040–1057

Macbeth was a hereditary ruler (mormaer) of Moray and nephew of Malcolm II. He proclaimed himself king after killing King Duncan, his cousin, in 1040 at Bathgowan, near Elgin. Duncan's sons, Malcolm (later Malcolm III Canmore) and Donald Bane, were both forced to flee. Malcolm sought refuge with his uncle Siward, Earl of Northumbria and Donald Bane fled to the Hebrides. Malcolm, with the support of Siward, raised an army against Macbeth and marched into Scotland in 1054. A battle was fought at Dunsinane, but it was not until three years later, at the battle of Lumphanan, that he finally defeated Macbeth and killed him. Macbeth's son, Lulach, by his wife, Gruoch, daughter of Kenneth III, succeeded his father to the throne for a brief period, but was killed by Malcolm, who took the throne in 1058.

The legends (much embellished) which were told over the years about King Macbeth were gathered by John of Fordun and Hector Boece and reproduced in the work of sixteenth century chronicler Holinshed. It was Holinshed's work that provided the source material for Shakespeare's play. Although Shakespeare portrays the king as a villain, Macbeth was merely a product of his time, a time in which all rulers struggled to gain power by whatever means necessary and to maintain it against constant threat of usurpation. Macbeth's reign was a reasonably prosperous one. He was buried on the island of Iona.

MacCAIG, NORMAN
(1910–96)
POET

Although he was born, grew up, and lived in Scotland's capital, his mother's Hebridean origin was a great influence on MacCaig. She was from Scalpay, Harris, and boyhood visits there made a deep impression. MacCaig attended the Royal High School and then Edinburgh University, where he studied Classics. Much of his working life was spent as a primary school teacher, interrupted by World War II, when conscientious objections to fighting meant that he spent time in various prisons and doing landwork. In 1967 he became the first Fellow in Creative Writing at Edinburgh University, and he later held a similar post while teaching at the University of Stirling.

MacCaig's poetry began as part of the 'New Apocalypse' movement, a surrealist mode of writing, and his first collection, *Far Cry*, was published in 1943. *Riding Lights* in 1965 marked a complete break, to formal, metrical, clear expression, always in modern English. Two main locales feature in his work: Edinburgh, his native city, and his holiday home of Assynt, in north-west Sutherland, where MacCaig spent much time, especially in the summer months. MacCaig's fame spread steadily in his later years, and his honours included the OBE and the Queen's Medal for Poetry. No Scottish poetry anthology would be complete without a selection of his work.

MACDIARMID, HUGH (CHRISTOPHER MURRAY GRIEVE)
(1892–1978)
Nationalist poet

Born Christopher Murray Grieve, in Langholm, Dumfriesshire, the man who was to become known as Hugh MacDiarmid attended Langholm Academy before moving to Edinburgh to train as a teacher at Broughton Junior Student Centre (Broughton High School). In 1911, he moved into journalism, finding his first job at the *Edinburgh Evening Despatch*. When World War I broke out, he joined the Royal Army Medical Corps. During this period, he wrote both prose and verse and, already committed to the cause of Scottish Nationalism, determined to become a nationalist poet. After the war, he married Peggy Skinner and they settled in Montrose in 1921, where he continued to write, and edited anthologies of Scottish poetry and prose writing, including *The Scottish Chapbook*, in which some of his own work featured. He also became a founder member of the National Party of Scotland (which became the Scottish National Party). As Hugh MacDiarmid, he took up the cause of Scottish culture, writing poetry in Scots and promoting Scots as a valid contemporary literary language. Two volumes of his verse, *Sangschaw* and *Penny Wheep*, were published in 1925 and 1926 respectively and his most acclaimed work, dedicated to FG Scott, his former English teacher at Langholm, *A Drunk Man Looks at the Thistle*, was published in 1926.

The success of *A Drunk Man Looks at the Thistle* was followed by a rather bleak period in MacDiarmid's life. He went to London and there his marriage fell apart. *To Circumjack Cenrastus*, his next major work, did not live up to his expectations. He then met his second wife, Valda, and moved to Whalsay in 1933, where his writing muse seemed to return with renewed vigour. In this period, he joined the Communist Party, from 1934 to 1939. During World War II, MacDiarmid worked in a munitions factory in Glasgow. In 1951, he moved to Biggar in Lanarkshire. His active interest in Communism was regenerated, and he rejoined the party in 1957. He stood, unsuccessfully, as Communist candidate for West Perthshire and Kinross in 1964. He died in Edinburgh.

Other works of Hugh MacDiarmid include *Hymns to Lenin* (1931, 1932, 1957), *Scots Unbound* (1932), and *A Kist o' Whistles* (1947). His autobiography, *Lucky Poet: A Self-Study in Literature and Political Ideas*, was published in 1943.

MACDONALD, FLORA
(1722–1790)
JACOBITE HEROINE

Flora Macdonald was born on the island of South Uist in the Hebrides. Her father died when she was very young and she was adopted by Lady Clanranald. She spent some time in Edinburgh completing her education before returning to Skye to live. Whilst visiting relatives on Uist in 1746, she became involved in a daring plot to smuggle Bonnie Prince Charlie, who was in hiding in the Outer Hebrides after his defeat at Culloden, to Skye. Disguised as Flora's Irish maid and going by the name of 'Betty Burke', the prince sailed with Flora's party to Skye. Narrowly avoiding capture by government troops, Flora successfully smuggled him to Portree. The prince escaped and left his rescuer with a gold locket with his portrait inside as a gesture of gratitude. Flora's part in the prince's escape was discovered and she was arrested and taken to London, where she was imprisoned in the Tower. She was eventually released in 1747 and allowed to return to Skye. In 1750, she married Allan Macdonald of Kingsburgh. In 1773, Samuel Johnson and James Boswell travelled to Skye to meet her and were impressed by her fine looks and her gentle manner.

In 1774, Flora and Allan emigrated to America, where Allan fought for the British in the American War of Independence until he was taken prisoner. Flora returned to Scotland in 1779 and her husband followed her two years later. They lived together at Kingsburgh until 1790, when Flora died.

MACDONALD, MARGARET
(1865–1933)
See Mackintosh, Charles Rennie

MACDONALD, JAMES RAMSAY
(1866–1937)
LABOUR POLITICIAN AND PRIME MINISTER OF GREAT BRITAIN

Ramsay MacDonald, the illegitimate son of Ann Ramsay, a maidservant, was born in Lossiemouth in Morayshire. He attended a local board school, and after some years became a pupil-teacher. In addition to his formal education, MacDonald increased his knowledge considerably through his love of books.

In 1884, he moved to London, where he met and married Margaret Ethel Gladstone. Once in London he began to take an increasingly active part in the Labour movement. In 1900 he became secretary of the Independent Labour Party. He served on London County Council from 1901 to 1904 and in 1906 stood for parliament, and was elected MP for Leicester. His skill as a speaker and his leadership qualities were recognised within the Parliamentary Labour Party and he became Chairman in 1911. In 1914, he resigned this position because of his opposition to Great Britain's entry into World War I. In 1918, he lost his parliamentary seat, but in 1922 he was returned to the House of Commons once more, as MP for Aberavon, in 1922. In this year also, he was appointed Leader of the Labour Party.

In 1924, the first Labour government in the history of Great Britain came into being, with Ramsay MacDonald as Prime Minister and Foreign Secretary. The government was a minority one and short-lived;

it lasted less than a year. In 1929, Labour came into power again, this time with a majority, and MacDonald led this government until 1931, during which time he visited the United States of America, the first British Prime Minister to do so. In the summer of 1931, with the economic depression becoming increasingly serious, MacDonald resigned as Prime Minister. In spite of the opposition of his own party, who saw the move as a betrayal and reacted by removing him from his position as party chairman, he immediately formed a coalition with the Conservatives. This coalition held power from 1931 to 1935 and instituted a programme of economic reform.

In 1935, MacDonald resigned as premier. Stanley Baldwin took over and MacDonald served as Lord President of the Council. Two years later, MacDonald died.

MCGONAGALL, WILLIAM

(1830–1902)

Poet

William McGonagall was born in Edinburgh, and spent his childhood in the Orkney islands and in Dundee. His father was an Irish weaver and passed on his skills to his son. McGonagall worked as a weaver in Dundee, and devoted his spare time to his interests in the theatre, acting as an enthusiastic amateur in the city's Theatre Royal. He also took up writing verse and had an unshakeable faith in his skills as a poet. His first collection of poems was published in 1877 and he then embarked upon an itinerant existence, travelling throughout central Scotland, giving public readings of his verse and selling his work in broadsheet form. He acquired a certain amount of fame for his efforts, more for the amusement that his poems caused than for the poetic gift he believed he had. He travelled to England and to America in the 1880s and was bitterly disappointed when the accolades he sought were not forthcoming, and returned to Dundee with hardly a penny to his name. A collection of his verse, *Poetic Gems*, was published in 1890, and although his dreams of becoming Poet Laureate were never realised, his unique brand of enthusiastic doggerel won him an affectionate following. McGonagall has been called 'The World's Worst Poet' and some of his verses, such as 'The Railway Bridge Over the Silvery Tay', which was published in his first collection, have become classics of their own unique genre.

A third collection of his work, *More Poetic Gems*, was published posthumously, in 1962.

McGREGOR, EWAN GORDON
(1971–)
Actor

Both his parents were teachers, but Ewan McGregor was not an enthusiastic pupil at Morrison's Academy in his home town, Crieff. He left at sixteen to be a stagehand at Perth Theatre, about twenty miles away, where he learned many practical skills before doing a year's foundation course in drama at Kirkcaldy College of Technology. He went on to the Guildhall School of Music and Drama in London. TV and film roles came quickly, the most notable being his role as Alex in Danny Boyle's *Shallow Grave* before his performance as Renton in Boyle's film of Irvine Welsh's *Trainspotting* (1996) for which he won a Scottish BAFTA. After that he was in even more demand and proved his versatility in a wide range of roles, from a glam rock singer in *Velvet Goldmine* (1998) to James Joyce in *Nora* (2000). In 2003 he won a Scottish BAFTA for his performance in *Young Adam*.

In 1999, 2002 and 2005, McGregor starred as the young Obi-Wan Kenobi in *Star Wars* Episodes 1,2 and 3. The role may not have stretched his acting abilities but it brought him even wider fame around the world.

He also combined with others in the Natural Nylon film production company.

In 1995 MacGregor married Eve Mavrakis, a French production designer, and they have three daughters, one of whom is adopted. He has always liked bikes and, with his friend Charlie Boorman, has made two long-range journeys which have been the subject of books and films, from London to New York via Siberia and North America, and from John o' Groats to Cape Town. McGregor and his family are now based in California.

MACKENZIE, SIR ALEXANDER
(*c*.1760–1820)
FUR TRADER AND EXPLORER

Scots were prominent in the development of modern

Canada, not only as politicians and businessmen but as trappers and traders in the fur trade which flourished from the 17th to the 20th centuries. Alexander Mackenzie was born in Stornoway, Lewis, and was taken to New York at the age of ten when his father emigrated there. In 1778 he was living with relatives in Montreal and joined a fur-trading company in the following year. Rivalry between fur traders was pushing out the frontiers and Mackenzie made two epic journeys, the first in 1789 down the great river which bears his name, to the Arctic Ocean; the second in 1792–3 when he completed the first overland crossing of Canada to the Pacific shore. In 1799 he returned to Great Britain, wrote an account of his *Voyages* (1801) and was knighted in 1802. A wealthy man, he married a 14-year old heiress of his own clan, Geddes Mackenzie, and purchased her ancestral estate of Avoch in Ross-shire. There he built a harbour, setting it up as a fishing port. Mackenzie was typical of many Scots colonials and 'nabobs' who returned to invest in and reinvigorate the 'old country'.

MACKINTOSH, CHARLES RENNIE
(1868–1928), **AND MARGARET MACDONALD MACKINTOSH**
(1865–1933)
ARCHITECT AND DESIGNER

Charles Rennie Mackintosh was born in Glasgow, where he attended Allan Glen's School. He then started an architectural apprenticeship under the architect John Hutchison, supplementing his practical experience with night classes at Glasgow School of Art. In 1889, when Mackintosh's apprenticeship was over, he went to work for the firm of Honeyman and Kepple as a draughtsman. At the art school, he made the acquaintance of Herbert Macnair, with whom he was to work quite closely. It was here that he also met his future wife Margaret Macdonald whom he also found to be an artistic kindred spirit.

Margaret Macdonald was born in Staffordshire. She and her sister Frances went to study at Glasgow School of Art and it was here that she was introduced by Fra Newbery, headmaster of the school, to Charles Rennie Mackintosh. Margaret, Frances, Charles Rennie Mackintosh and Herbert Macnair, whom Frances married, became collectively known as 'The Four', exponents of a style that came to be known as 'The Glasgow Style', related to Art Nouveau. In 1894, The Four exhibited together for the first time in the Glasgow School of Art Club Exhibition. Their creative output was very varied and included watercolours, metalwork and textiles, posters and furniture, illustration, glasswork and enamelwork. When they put their work on show in London at the Arts and Crafts Society Exhibition in 1896, they found themselves at the receiving end of much criticism, which centred upon the new style of their work.

Margaret and Frances shared a studio and worked particularly closely together from 1896 to 1899, when Frances left Glasgow with Macnair. Margaret's work during her period with Frances is particularly memorable for her watercolours and stained glass designs. Sensuous, organic shapes, ghostly figures and plant-based patterns are common elements.

From 1899 Macdonald began to work in close collaboration with Charles Rennie Mackintosh and in 1900 they married. Macdonald's work featured in many of the interiors Mackintosh designed and had a less ethereal quality: painted panels in furniture or on walls, designed for the part the played in the whole scheme rather than for their individual effect. While Great Britain had not been ready to welcome the work of The Four, they found much more success when they ventured into Europe. Macdonald and Mackintosh were invited to exhibit their work in the Vienna Secession Exhibition of 1900, and were given a wonderful reception. Two years later, in Turin, Margaret won the Diploma of Honour at the International Exhibition there.

Mackintosh's output as an architect was not prolific, and it was not as well received in Great Britain as it might have been, but it had a strong influence in Europe. Although his designs were very stylised and showed some of the characteristics of Art Nouveau, his emphasis on bold straight lines in his work was a departure from the more sensuous curves so typical of Art Nouveau. His wife Margaret collaborated with him on some of his projects, contributing to the interior decoration of some of the buildings he worked on. The buildings that he designed – Glasgow School of Art; Queen's Cross Church in Maryhill, Glasgow; Scotland Street School in Kingston, Glasgow; Martyr's Public School, Parson Street, Glasgow; Miss Catherine Cranston's Willow Tea Rooms, Sauchiehall Street, Glasgow, and Hill House, Helensburgh – all bore a style that was undeniably Scottish, modern and Mackintosh. The design was complete, from exterior structure to furniture, fittings and decorative detail. In Glasgow School of Art even the easels which the students used were designed by Mackintosh. So important was the vision of the design as an integral whole, that sometimes comfort and practicality were sacrificed for the sake of it. The severely vertical high-backed chairs for which Mackintosh has become well-known, for example, were clearly designed for their visual impact rather than for their comfort.

In 1913 Mackintosh left Scotland for Chelsea and apart from one further architectural project in Northampton in 1917, concentrated his efforts on textile design and painting. From 1920, he lived in France and concentrated on his watercolours. In the autumn of 1927 he returned to London on medical advice after being diagnosed as having cancer of the throat and tongue. He died on December 10 1928. Although his work was widely acclaimed in Europe and especially in Germany, Mackintosh never achieved the same level of success in Great Britain during his lifetime. Appreciation of the contribution he made to British architecture and design has grown considerably in the years since his death. Margaret Macdonald died on January 10 1933.

MCLAREN, BILL

(1925–)

RUGBY COMMENTATOR

Bill McLaren was born and brought up in Hawick. His love of rugby began when he was young, and as a pupil at Hawick High School, he played for the first fifteen from the age of fifteen. When he was seventeen, he played his first game as wing-forward for Hawick.

In 1942, McLaren was called up for army service and joined the Royal Artillery as an officer trainee. He served in Africa and Italy during the war, and he played rugby for his regiment and also for the Central Mediterranean Forces rugby club. He left the army in 1947 and took up teaching, but continued to play for Hawick, with the hope of a place in the Scotland team. In 1947, he captained the Hawick Seven. However, he was diagnosed with tuberculosis in 1948 and the illness finished his career as a player. When he recovered two years later, he started work as a sports reporter on the *Hawick Express*. This led to a commentary audition with BBC Radio, and he was invited to give his first radio commentary in 1952. In 1953, he took part in his first international commentary in the match between Wales and Scotland. In the 1960s, he was asked to move into television and adapted to the change readily.

McLaren continued to work for the BBC and established a reputation as a highly knowledgeable and scrupulously unbiased commentator with a genuine love of the sport. A particular high point in his career came when Scotland won the Grand Slam in 1990, when he was commentator during Scotland's momentous victory over England at Murrayfield. In 1991, he was asked to move to Independent Television to cover the World Cup, but he refused, preferring to remain with the BBC.

In 2000, after forty years in broadcasting, Bill McLaren, 'The Voice of Rugby', was given a special award, the Freedom of Scottish Rugby, by the Scottish Rugby Union. The occasion was made all the more joyous by another momentous match at Murrayfield, Scotland beating England 19–11 in the Calcutta Cup and denying them the chance of the Grand Slam and the Triple Crown.

MACLEAN, ALISTAIR
(1922–87)
NOVELIST

A son of the manse, Maclean was born in Glasgow but spent his childhood at Daviot in Inverness-shire, attending Inverness Royal Academy before his father was transferred back to Glasgow. There he went to Hillhead High School and Glasgow University. He served in the Royal Navy from 1941–46, much of the time as a torpedo operator on destroyers in the 'Arctic Convoys' to Murmansk. From 1946 he became a teacher at Gallowflat School, Rutherglen. After winning a short story competition in the *Glasgow Herald*, he was encouraged to write more fiction, and his first novel, *HMS Ulysses*, was published in 1955 and became an immediate best-seller. A string of others followed, with *The Guns of Navarone*, *Ice Station Zebra*, and *Where Eagles Dare*. In all he wrote thirty-two books, of which twenty-six were novels. Maclean never claimed literary status and from 1963 lived a somewhat nomadic life, never settling in one place for long. In 1953 he married his first wife Gisela Heinrichsen; they had two sons and adopted a third, but were divorced in 1972, in which year he married Marcelle Georgeus, but that ended in divorce in 1977. Maclean's life was complicated by heavy drinking, with subsequent regrets and guilt. His last eight years were spent in a rented villa on the Adriatic, near Dubrovnik. He died in the University Hospital in Munich, Germany, while on holiday with his first wife.

MACLEAN, JOHN
(1879–1923)
Socialist campaigner

John Maclean was born in Pollokshaws, Glasgow. He attended Pollokshaws Academy and Queen's Park School before progressing to Glasgow University. He began his career as a teacher in Govan but was soon advised that he was ill-suited to the job.

Maclean's interest in Socialism had begun at an early age and he joined the Social Democratic Federation in the early 1900s. A strict teetotaller, clean-living to the point of self-denial, he dedicated most of his life to the promotion of his Socialist beliefs and to displays of his own conviction in those beliefs. He gave regular public talks on Marxist theory and was very successful in converting many workers to the cause of Socialism, becoming a leading voice of Red Clydeside. His vociferous public opposition to World War I caused him to be arrested three times in the period between 1915 and 1918. His sentence in 1918 was for five years, but Maclean claimed that prison food was poisoned and went on hunger strike. His protests at being force-fed led to a public outcry and his release was secured after a few months. He was clearly weakened after his spell in prison, and continued to show signs of mental disturbance. Whether his increasing paranoia was triggered by the hardships of prison life, or was simply a manifestation of existing mental illness, will never be known.

After the war was over, Maclean remained determined to preach his beliefs, no matter what the consequence. Convinced that the way ahead lay in Scotland's independence as a worker's republic, he broke away from the British Socialist Party and the new Communist Party of Great Britain and set up the Scottish Worker's Party. His extreme radicalism and the obvious deterioration of his mental health isolated him further; support was dwindling, but he maintained his uncompromising stance, in spite of three further arrests between 1921 and 1923. In 1923, he stood as a parliamentary candidate for the Gorbals constituency, but his general physical condition had suffered considerably in the preceding years and the strain of the campaign took its toll on a body that was already very weak. He died in November 1923.

MACLEAN, SORLEY (SOMHAIRLE MACGILL-EAIN)
(1911–96)
POET

Oscaig, on Raasay, where Sorley Maclean was born and grew up, was steeped in the traditions of Gaelic song and music; his father, a tailor, was a singer and Sorley's brother John became a fine piper. The family were strict Calvinists and Sabbatarians – an influence that Maclean might have found deeply oppressive but which (though he escaped from it) he turned to constructive use, with the great debate between Free Will and Predestination giving his poetry much of its creative strength and tension. After school on Raasay and at Portree, he went to Edinburgh University, then to Moray House College of Education. He was already writing poetry in both English and Gaelic and was profoundly affected by his introduction to Hugh MacDiarmid's poems in 1933. MacDiarmid and he became close friends. His own poetic maturity began with a Gaelic poem, 'An Corra-Ghritheach', 'The Heron', in 1932. In 1934 he became a teacher at Portree High School, then at Plockton High School in Wester Ross, where he was headmaster until 1972. Despite this comparative isolation, the international political themes of the 1930s echo in his first collection, in *Dàin do Eimhir agus dàin eile* ('Poems to Eimhir and Other Poems'). Maclean fused the musicality and traditional themes of Gaelic (Eimhir was the wife of the legendary Cú Chulainn) with a modern sensibility and modern topics. He despised most of the Gaelic poetry of the 19th century, and even more the 'Celtic Twilight' of writers like 'Fiona Macleod' in the early 20th century.

Conscripted into the army in 1940, Maclean served in North Africa, being wounded three times, and invalided out after the battle of El Alamein in 1942. He continued to work on *An Cuilithionn,* 'The Cuillin', a meditative work on human suffering and human heroism. In 1946 he married Renee Stewart Cameron and they had three daughters. He died at Inverness and is buried at Portree, on Skye. Maclean is generally accepted as the finest Gaelic poet of the 20th century and a writer of international stature. Analysis and exploration of his work is still very much in progress.

MACMILLAN, KIRKPATRICK
(1813–1878)
INVENTOR OF THE BICYCLE

Kirkpatrick Macmillan was born in Dumfriesshire, near Thornhill. He worked for some time as a farm labourer before setting up in trade as a blacksmith at Keir Mill. He was regarded as a loveable eccentric in the village, and caused some amusement when he first began experimenting with the possibility of pedal-driven transport. After initial experiments with a three-wheel pedal-driven machine, he finally succeeded, in 1839, in building the first pedal-driven bicycle, a cumbersome construction with wooden wheels, but a working machine nonetheless.

He proved the efficiency of his invention by riding it on short local journeys initially. Then he rode it all the way from Keir to Glasgow, a distance of some seventy miles, causing quite a sensation. Macmillan did not patent his invention, and so never realised the commercial potential that it had, but the value of his work was soon recognised by others. His design was copied widely, and sadly Macmillan was not always acknowledged as the inventor. A copy of Macmillan's original machine now stands in the Museum of Transport in Glasgow and the smithy where he lived bears a plaque in commemoration of his life.

McRAE, COLIN STEELE
(1968–2007)
RALLY DRIVER

Rallying was a McRae family activity. McRae's father Jimmy was a five-times British champion and his brother Alister is also a rally driver. Born in Lanark, he began on trial bikes but by sixteen had moved on to cars and in 1986 entered the Scottish Rally Championship. His first international competition was the Swedish Rally (1987) and in 1991 he turned professional, becoming British Rally Champion that year and again in 1992. His first World Rally title was won in 1993 in Rally New Zealand, with Subaru, and from then on he was among the world's top drivers. From 1999–2002 he drove for Ford, and victory in the Safari Rally in 2002 made him, for a time, the driver with most event wins in the World Rally Championship. After a short stint with Citroën in 2003, McRae was no longer involved with a single works team. He participated in other racing series including the Le Mans 24 Hours and participated in the 2004 and 2005 Dakar Rallies. He was also working on the McRae R4, a car design intended to be cheaper and more versatile than the World Rally Car specification. It was introduced in 2006. On 15 September 2007, the lives of McRae, his five-year old son Johnny and two family friends, were brought to a tragically premature end when his helicopter crashed close to his home near Lanark.

MARGARET, SAINT
(*c.* 1046–1093)
Queen of Scotland

Margaret was born in Hungary. Her father was Edward the Aetheling (Edward the Exile), who had sought refuge in Hungary at the court of King Stephen. Edward Aetheling went back to England with Margaret and his son Edgar the Aetheling, hoping to claim the throne after the death of Edward the Confessor, but he died soon after reaching England. Edgar was denied the chance to claim the throne in place of his father, and he and Margaret were forced to flee to Scotland in 1066. Their ship landed in Fife. Margaret became married to Malcolm III Canmore, in Dunfermline, in 1070. The marriage was, by all accounts, a loving one.

Margaret was an educated, pious and refined woman

who brought much influence to bear both on her husband and his people. She introduced the English language to the Scottish court, and thereafter to a large area of the Scottish Lowlands. She organised the church into territorial divisions, ruled by bishops, and brought Benedictine monks to Dunfermline, where an abbey was founded. She is also thought to have ordered the building of St Margaret's Chapel on the Castle Rock in Edinburgh for her own use.

Margaret and Malcolm had six sons and two daughters. Three of their sons, Edgar, Alexander I and David I, became kings of Scotland. Margaret died very shortly after Malcolm in 1093.

MARY, QUEEN OF SCOTS
(1542–1587)
Tragic Queen

Mary Stewart was born in Linlithgow Palace in December 1952. Her father, James V of Scotland, died when she was one week old and she became Queen. She was betrothed in 1543 to Edward, son of Henry VIII and when the arrangement was repudiated, the English invaded Scotland in 1544 to 1545 ('The Rough Wooing'). The French agreed to help the Scots on condition that Mary was sent to France and there, in 1558, she married the young dauphin, Francis. He died in 1560. His mother, Catherine de Medici, now held power and she was no ally of Mary. Mary returned to Scotland in 1561. Elizabeth I was now on the English throne and the government of Scotland was led by

Protestants. The Roman Catholic church hoped that Mary would revive Roman Catholicism and make a claim on the English throne.

But Mary's attempts to revive the power of Roman Catholicism in Scotland were in vain and she had to allow her Protestant half-brother, the Earl of Moray, to assume the position of First Minister and to give several Protestant nobles prominent positions in her court in order to gain acceptance with her people. She, however, continued to practise Roman Catholicism, and her second husband, Henry Stewart, Lord Darnley, was also a Catholic. The marriage sparked off a revolt, led by Moray, which Mary successfully quelled.

The marriage to Darnley was not happy and when Mary's secretary, David Rizzio was murdered by Darnley and others in 1566, their relationship deteriorated further. A brief reconciliation following the birth of their son, James (who would be James VI of Scotland and James I of England), came to nothing. Darnley left Mary's court, but when he fell ill in 1566, she had him brought back to Kirk o' Field.

The house was blown up and Darnley was murdered. Both Mary and the Earl of Bothwell were suspected. Bothwell carried Mary off to Dunbar and married her and the anger of the Scottish nobles turned on them both. In June, 1567, Mary's forces were defeated at Carberry Hill. Bothwell fled and Mary surrendered to the insurgent lords.

She was imprisoned at Loch Leven Castle. Evidence (whether fabricated or genuine) was produced to establish her guilt in Darnley's murder, and she was forced to abdicate in favour of her infant son. The Earl of Moray was appointed Regent.

One year later, Mary escaped and gathered a force to challenge the Earl of Moray. But she was defeated at the Battle of Langside and fled to England, hoping to find sympathy with Elizabeth. Elizabeth made her a virtual prisoner and over the next eighteen years, Mary's name was associated with several pro-Catholic plots to depose Elizabeth. Finally, when Mary was living in Fotheringay Castle, a conspiracy to assassinate Elizabeth, organised by Anthony Babington, was uncovered. Mary was accused of having been part of the conspiracy and she was tried in October 1586. One year later, her execution warrant was signed by Elizabeth and with great calm and dignity, she went to her execution.

In spite of the many trials and tribulations she faced in her life, evidence points to the fact that Mary was an intelligent and charismatic woman who faced her difficulties, and ultimately her untimely and cruel death, with great courage.

MAXWELL, JAMES CLERK
(1831–79)
Physicist

Born in Edinburgh, Maxwell grew up into a scientifically enquiring teenager (his family called his experiments 'Jamsie's dirts') just as the 'new' sciences were emerging from the overall embrace of Natural Philosophy. He studied at Edinburgh Academy and University, and Cambridge, then became professor of Mathematics at Aberdeen when still only 26. He found the University there rather a serious place, complaining that no-one ever told jokes.

He transferred to London and then returned to Cambridge as its first professor of Experimental Physics. In 1873 he published a major *Treatise on Electricity and Magnetism*, which supplied the mathematical basis to Faraday's theory of electrical and magnetic forces. His greatest achievement, which establishes him as a vital predecessor of Albert Einstein, was his theory of electromagnetic radiation. Maxwell's discoveries of the subtleties of the physical universe never shook his strong belief in a divine creation; in fact, as in his famous comment on the identical nature of molecules across the universe, it confirmed it.

MITCHELL, JAMES LESLIE (LEWIS GRASSIC GIBBON)
(1901–1935)
NOVELIST

James Leslie Mitchell was born in Auchterless, Aberdeenshire. His father was a farmer. He attended Arbuthnot School and Mackie Academy. In 1917, he left school and went to Aberdeen to work as a journalist. He worked for a spell in Glasgow, writing for the *Scottish Farmer*, but following his dismissal from this post he abandoned journalism and enlisted in the Royal Army Service Corps. He served for more than three years abroad, in the Middle East, Egypt and India, and was discharged in 1923. He then took up employment as a clerk in the Royal Air Force, remaining in this job until 1929.

Mitchell began writing in the late 1920s and his experiences abroad contributed to his first books. In 1928, he published his first book, *Hanno, or the Future of Exploration*, which was followed by the novel *Stained Radiance* in 1930. *The Calends of Cairo*, published in 1931, was a work of nonfiction. Three more books followed in quick succession; *The Thirteenth Disciple* (1931), *Three Go Back* (1932) and *The Lost Trumpet* (1932). His best-known and most highly acclaimed work, *Sunset Song*, was also published in 1932, the first part of a trilogy, *A Scots Quair*. The second and third books in the trilogy, *Cloud Howe* and *Grey Granite* were published in 1933 and 1934 respectively. *A Scots Quair* traces the life of a young girl, Chris Guthrie, from her rural childhood in Aberdeenshire through major changes in her life and environment, and is set in the period including World War I and the Depression.

The trilogy, and in particular *Sunset Song*, is widely recognised as an important and influential work of twentieth-century Scottish literature. *A Scots Quair* was published under Mitchell's pseudonym of Lewis Grassic Gibbon. Two non-fictional works, a biography of MUNGO PARK, and *The Conquest of the Maya* were published in addition to *Grey Granite* in 1934.

Mitchell died in 1935, following an operation on a perforated gastric ulcer. His career as a writer had been brief, but brilliant. An unfinished novel, *The Speak of the Mearns,* was published many years after his death.

MONTGOMERIE, COLIN STUART
(1963–)
GOLFER

Born in Troon, Ayrshire, his father's job meant that the young Montgomerie's boyhood was largely spent in Yorkshire, though he attended Strathallan School in Perthshire for a time. Golf was the centre of his existence from early on and his talent for the game was quickly recognised. He won the Scottish Youth Championship in 1983 and the Scottish Amateur Championship in 1987, turning professional in the following year. His Ryder Cup debut was in 1991 and he has been a dominant figure in that tournament ever since. By 1993 he was ranked as Europe's No. 1 golfer and held that position for seven years. In 1994 he moved into the top ten of the World Rankings and since then has ranked amongst the world's best golfers.

Consistency in performance has always been the hallmark of Montgomerie's game. Despite many impressive victories, though, Monty, as he is known, has never won a major championship, coming second five times; in 2006 he failed to win the US Open by a single stroke. His career went through a difficult patch in the early 2000s, culminating in divorce from his wife Eimear in 2006. The couple had three children. In 2008 he married Gaynor Knowles. He is due to captain the Ryder Cup team in 2010.

MORGAN, EDWIN

(1920–)

POET

Edwin Morgan was born and brought up in Glasgow. His father worked for a company of iron and steel merchants. Morgan was educated at Rutherglen Academy and Glasgow High School before progressing to Glasgow University. He was quite a solitary and introverted young man, and had been a voracious reader since childhood. Although he was academically more than equal to the rigours of university life, he was not entirely happy there and was prone to depression. The outbreak of war interrupted his studies and he registered as a conscientious objector, then opted for service in the Royal Army Medical Corps as a clerk and stretcher bearer. When the war was over, he returned to university and graduated with first class honours in English, after which he took up a post as a lecturer. His first collection of poems was published in 1952 and was entitled *The Vision of Cathkin Braes*. In the same year he published the first of many translations: a translation of *Beowolf*.

Morgan's early work was in many ways a reflection of his state of mind at the time. Having become aware of his homosexuality at an early age, he found the necessity of keeping such a secret (for secret it had to be in those days) very painful. His clandestine love-life had not been a happy one and he was deeply troubled by feelings of pessimism and guilt. A marked change in his work was effected when Morgan finally found himself in a happy relationship with John Scott, in the early 1960s. They were together almost until the time of Scott's death in 1978, and the gloomy tone of Morgan's earlier work became replaced with verses that contained optimism and a sense of gladness of being. In 1968, a second collection of verse was published, *A Second Life*, which contained poems which displayed Morgan's fascination with the changing face of Glasgow in the 1960s, and the theme of change was to run through much of his work in later years. His poetry is wide-ranging in both style (from medieval to ultramodern) and subject (love and eroticism, urban people and life, science fiction). Morgan was a dedicated teacher, and he remained at Glasgow University, where he became Titular Professor of English in 1975, until he retired in 1980. During this period and since then, his creative output has been considerable and he has been honoured with several awards in recognition of his work as a poet, critic and translator. In 1982, the year in which a collection of verse entitled *Poems of Thirty Years* was published, he received an OBE.

MUIR, JOHN
(1838–1914)
Conservationist

John Muir was born in Dunbar, in East Lothian. He moved with his family to the United States of America in 1849 and studied at the University of Wisconsin. He was passionately interested in natural history and in particular in botany, and he explored and studied the Yosemite area in the years between 1868 and 1874. From 1876 to 1879 he took part in the United States Geodetic Survey, during which he sighted a glacier in Alaska which was named after him.

Muir realised the importance of preserving wild areas of countryside and was a dedicated conservationist with a vision ahead of his time. In 1890, a long and persistent campaign conducted by him was finally successful in gaining the approval of Congress to declare the Yosemite Valley as a National Park. In 1892, he started the Sierra Club, with the aim of fostering a concern for the conservation of the Sierra Nevada. He continued his crusade, and during his life he was responsible for around 150 million acres of forest and wilderness being designated as national parkland. He also travelled widely, visiting countries all around the world to carry out studies on forest land and to advise on forestry management, and he wrote a number of books which include *The Mountains of California* (1894), *Our National Parks* (1901) and *The Yosemite* (1912).

The work of John Muir was only recognised much later in the land of his birth. In 1984, The John Muir Trust was set up to for the purpose of purchasing and conserving wild land. Near Dunbar, where he was born, a coastal country park and nature reserve has been named after him.

MUNGO, SAINT

(*c.*520–*c.*612)
See St Kentigern.

MUNRO, SIR HUGH THOMAS
(1856–1919)
Mountaineer and Topographer

Born in London, into a wealthy Scottish family with a country estate at Lindertis near Kirriemuir, Munro's love of mountains began when he first visited the Alps at the age of 17. His parents had intended a business career for him, but he joined the army, serving in South Africa in campaigns against the Basutos. On his return he became manager of the family estate, which he inherited, along with his baronetcy, in 1913. He married in 1892 but his wife died in 1902, leaving him with four young children.

A prominent member of the Scottish Mountaineering Club (SMC), Munro was elected as Honorary President in 1894, participating with equal enjoyment in hill expeditions and social gatherings. His feeling for the mountains took two forms: most famously as the man who 'measured' them. In Munro's day there was no general agreement about which were peaks and in many cases the exact height was uncertain. With compass, aneroid barometer, and measuring poles, Munro painstakingly paced the slopes. Most of his work was done alone, sometimes in secret if on the land of someone who would have objected.

In 1889 his project was adopted officially by the SMC: to assemble a list of all summits of 3000 feet or more. 'Munro's Tables' were published from 1891, and his name is firmly linked to the 280-plus summits, as 'Munros'. His other side was non-scientific: he was a firm believer in the supernatural and claimed to have heard 'heavenly music' while walking in the hills. Munro died of pneumonia, in Tarascon, southern France, where he had helped to set up a Red Cross canteen.

MURRAY, ANDREW (ANDY)
(1987–)
Tennis Player

Andy Murray was born in Dunblane, Perthshire, and started playing with bat and ball at the age of three. He entered his first tennis tournament at five. In 1995, as an eight-year-old, he was a pupil at the local primary school when a deranged gunman entered and killed sixteen children and a teacher. As a schoolboy he was intensely sporty and competitive, in football and boxing as well as tennis, but he chose to pursue tennis and went to Florida to win the Orange Bowl tournament in 1999. At fifteen he went to the Sanchez-Casal academy in Barcelona.

In 2004 he won the US Open Boys' Championship and in 2005 became the youngest player ever to represent Britain in the Davis Cup. Turning professional that year, he reached the third round of the Wimbledon tournament. In February 2006 he won his first major title, at San Jose, California and was acknowledged as the British No. 1 player. A year later he and his brother Jamie became the first siblings to win the single and the men's doubles titles at San Jose. By then, Murray was firmly established among the top players in the Grand Slam competition. With five title wins in the 2008 season, he was placed 4th in the world ATP rankings.

He started 2009 well, beating world No. 1 Roger Federer and world No. 2 Rafael Nadal to win the 2009 Capitala World Tennis Championship in Abu Dabi. He also triumphed at the ABN AMRO Tournament in Rotterdam.

MURRAY, CHARLES (CHIC)
(1919–1985)
COMEDIAN AND ENTERTAINER

Chic Murray was born in Greenock. He was the only child of William and Isabella Murray. His father suffered from severe lung problems after having been gassed in the First World War, and died when Chic was fourteen. Chic was musical, with a fine singing voice. He learned to play the organ and the piano when he was young and became an accomplished musician. He was also able to play banjo and guitar. His talents as a comedian revealed themselves when he was at school, where he amused teachers and pupils with fantastic excuses for lateness. He left school aged fifteen to begin an apprenticeship in marine engineering on the Clyde, and in his spare time formed a band, The Whinbillies, with his friend Neilie McNeil. When war broke out, Chic was excused military service on medical grounds and went to work at Fairey Aviation in Essex. He was injured when the plant was bombed and six months later, was back in Greenock, working in his former job and playing in a three-piece band, Chic and His Chicks. In 1943, he met his future wife, Maidie, who was performing at the Greenock Empire. They were married in 1945.

Maidie, a professional performer with several years' experience, recognised Chic's talents. She persuaded him to work with her as a double act; both of them would sing, and Chic would also tell jokes and stories. In the following years they toured the theatres of Britain together with increasing success and performed in the United States and Australia.

Chic's comic talent was a major factor in their popularity and his meandering stories and bizarre humour rendered his audiences helpless with laughter. They had two children, Douglas and Annabelle, and bought two houses in Edinburgh's Bruntsfield Terrace to convert into a hotel.

Unfortunately, marriage to Chic was difficult. He could be very exasperating, was a notoriously erratic timekeeper, became over-fond of alcohol and had a number of affairs. Eventually, Maidie left him. Chic pursued his career alone, and the couple were divorced in 1972. Chic never recovered from the divorce and continued to be a frequent visitor at Maidie's home, even after she remarried.

Chic's solo career took him into television work in the 1970s, with a few minor appearances in films, but he never recovered the degree of success that he had enjoyed working in variety with Maidie. He continued to drink heavily and his health suffered. Then in the early 1980s, he played the headmaster in *Gregory's Girl* and his career took a turn for the better. Following the success of *Gregory's Girl*, he was offered roles in two more films; *Saigon – Year of the Cat* and *Scotch Myths*. Then in

1984, he was asked to play on stage in Liverpool as BILL SHANKLY in *You'll Never Walk Alone*. His performance was a resounding success.

Chic's health continued to deteriorate, however, and he died from a perforated ulcer in 1985. His funeral service was packed with figures from the entertainment industry who had come to know him and love him for (or in spite of) his unique character and his irreverent wit.

NAIRNE, LADY CAROLINA
(1766–1845)
WRITER OF SCOTTISH SONGS AND BALLADS

Lady Carolina Nairne, née Oliphant, was born in Gask in Perthshire. Her father was a Jacobite and her mother was descended from the Robertsons of Struan. She was married in 1806 to Major Nairne, who became Lord Nairne in 1824, and they lived in Edinburgh.

She was a lover of poetry and traditional music throughout her life and had a reputation as a poet and songwriter of great skill herself. She published nothing under her own name while she was alive, but a series of her songs, written to the tunes of traditional airs, was published under a pseudonym 'Mrs Bogan of Bogan' in the *Scottish Minstrel*.

After her death a great many more of her songs and ballads were published, several of which are still favourites with lovers of Scottish traditional music today. They include: 'Will Ye No' Come Back Again?' (the Jacobite lament for Bonnie Prince Charlie), 'Charlie

is My Darling' (another Jacobite song), 'Caller Herrin'',
'The Laird o' Cockpen' and 'The Land o' the Leal'.

NAPIER, JOHN
(1550–1617)
Mathematician

John Napier was born at Merchiston Castle in
Edinburgh and went to St Andrews University at the
age of thirteen. When he was eighteen, he became
the eighth Laird of Merchiston. He became an active
supporter of the Reformation Movement while he was
at St Andrews and he was a devoutly religious and strict
Protestant. In later years he was to publish some of
his religious writings, including *The Plaine Discovery of
the Whole Revelation of St John* (1593), an interpretation
of the Bible and a publication of some importance at
the time. He did not complete his studies at university,
but travelled in Europe for some time to broaden his
horizons before settling back home at Merchiston
where he pursued his interests in science in general and
in particular, in mathematics.

He is best remembered for inventing a system of
natural logarithms using base e, which, although it
was not the only such system to be under development
at the time, was the first one to be published, and he
described it in his work *Mirifici Logarithmorum Canonis
Descriptio* (1614). He also devised a calculating machine,
which used a set of numbered rods, called 'Napier's
Bones'. He described this device in the publication
Rabdologiae (1617). Napier was one of the first to use

the decimal point as it is used today in the writing of decimal fractions.

Mathematics was not the only science in which Napier took a lively interest, and he was a talented inventor. Among his inventions was an 'armoured chariot', something akin to a horse-drawn tank, which was devised as part of a proposed armoury against the military threat from Spain.

John Napier's former home at Merchiston has now become part of the sprawling campus of Napier University (formerly Napier College of Science and Technology).

OBREE, GRAEME
(1965–)
RACING CYCLIST

Born in Nuneaton, Warwickshire, Obree's life has been a mixture of triumphs, struggles and troubles. The family moved to Irvine, Ayrshire when he was very young, and as his autobiography, *The Flying Scotsman*, shows, he regards himself very much as a Scot. Depression and poor self-esteem clouded his teenage years, with two suicide attempts. An attempt to run a bicycle shop failed. But Obree clung to a vision, of breaking the world record for an hour's distance in a velodrome. On a bicycle designed and built by himself, 'Old Faithful', and adopting a riding position of his own invention, he broke the record on 17 July 1993, with 51.596 km at a velodrome in Hamar, Norway. A few days later, Chris Boardman achieved 52.27 km at Bordeaux.

Obree retook the record in April 1994 and held it until Miguel Indurain broke it in September that year. The *Union Cycliste Internationale* eventually banned Obree's riding position and its replacement, the 'Superman' style, with which which he won the World Pursuit Championship in 1995 on 'Old Faithful'. Obree won numerous other championships in the 1990s, despite a spell of severe depression and a further suicide attempt in 1994. He has always been an outspoken opponent of the 'drug culture' of international cycle racing, and frequently at odds with the sport's officialdom. *The Flying Scotsman* was published in 2003 and has also been made into a film.

PAGAN, ISOBEL
(*c.*1741–1821)
SHEBEEN KEEPER AND POET

'Tibbie' Pagan was born in New Cumnock, Ayrshire. Her story is a reminder of the struggle that independent-minded women had to lead a life that was not domestic or industrial drudgery. A clergyman once called her 'the most perfect realisation of a witch or hag that I ever saw'. In one of her poems she describes her education as 'ten weeks when I was seven years old'. She could read but not write, had a squint, a tumour on one side, and a deformed foot; and lived near Muirkirk in a hovel beside a tar-works, where she sold bad whisky and presided at gatherings of bonnet-lairds and farm-lads who came to drink and laugh at her jokes and insults. In this she resembled 'Poosie Nancy' of the Mauchline tavern, made famous by Burns. But she was also a poet in her own right. Her verses were transcribed by her friend William Gemmell, a tailor, and in 1805 were published in Glasgow as *Collection of Songs and Poems on Several Occasions*. Isobel Pagan died in Muirkirk and was buried in the churchyard there.

PARK, MUNGO
(1771–1806)
DOCTOR, EXPLORER

Mungo Park was born at Fowlshiels in the Borders. He studied medicine at Edinburgh University and after qualifying in 1791, went as assistant surgeon on a botany expedition to Sumatra. Shortly after his return, he successfully applied to lead an expedition organised by the Africa Association to find the source of the Niger. He set off from England to the Gambia in 1795, travelled inland from the Gambia with a few African companions, and reached the Niger in July 1796. The trip was a success and Park returned to Great Britain more than two years later, complete with maps that he had drawn of the upper Niger. But it had also been particularly arduous – he was taken prisoner by an Arab tribe during the course of it and he had suffered terribly from the heat and from the physical effort of navigating such difficult terrain.

After his return, he married and settled down to life in practice in Peebles. In 1804, he was given the chance to return to Africa at the head of another, bigger expedition and seized the opportunity eagerly.

Some forty men left on the expedition, but three-quarters of them died before they reached the Niger. Park struggled on as his party became further depleted, but disaster struck him and the other few who were left, as they tried to navigate the waters of the great river. Their boat came to grief in the rapids of Boussa when they were ambushed by local inhabitants and all of them lost their lives.

Mungo Park was a courageous man and a dedicated scientist, but he was also extremely modest about his achievements. His explorations were undertaken in his quest for knowledge, rather than with any desire for self-promotion. While he was living in Peebles, he made the acquaintance of SIR WALTER SCOTT and the two became firm friends. He published a journal of his first trip to the Niger, entitled *Travels in the Interior of Africa*, in 1799.

PATERSON, WILLIAM
(1658–1719)
FOUNDER OF THE BANK OF ENGLAND

William Paterson was born in Tinwald in Dumfriesshire, but was brought up in England. He went to the West Indies for a number of years, and although the precise means by which he acquired it is still a matter for speculation, (fair trade or piracy) he returned to Great Britain with a fortune. In 1691, back in London, he came up with the proposal for the founding of the Bank of England and when it eventually came into being in 1694, he was appointed one of the directors. It did not develop as he had thought so he resigned from his post in 1695 to return to Scotland to give his support as a fund-raiser for a scheme, backed by the Scottish Parliament, to start a Scottish company for trade with Africa and the Indies. Paterson then proposed the idea of starting a Scottish colony on Darien on the isthmus of Panama and committed himself to the project wholeheartedly. His family sailed with the first would-be settlers in 1698. The expedition was a disaster. One third of those who had set out failed to survive the voyage and when Paterson returned with the survivors only one year later, he had lost his wife and son, he was in extremely poor health and had suffered irretrievable financial loss. Some say the collapsed venture was, in part, due to English and Spanish intransigence although bad planning and disease were undoubtedly contributory factors.

In the following years, Paterson was deeply involved in the finance and trade aspects of the proposed union of the parliaments and when the united parliament sat for the first time in 1707, he took his seat in the House of Commons as MP for Dumfries burghs.

In 1715, Paterson was made an award of £18,000 as compensation for his financial losses in the Darien Scheme. He died four years later.

PEPLOE, SAMUEL JOHN
(1871–1935)
PAINTER

Samuel Peploe was born in Edinburgh. He began

studying at Edinburgh College of Art in 1891, and three years later went to the Académie Juian in Paris. It was the first of many visits to France and his experiences instilled in him a great admiration for the work of many of the contemporary French painters, such as Cézanne, Manet, Monet and later, Matisse. In 1903, he held his first exhibition in Great Britain. Peploe made the acquaintance of JD Fergusson, who had also been to France and had an equally high regard for the work of the Impressionists. Peploe, Fergusson, and fellow painters Leslie Hunter and FC Cadell, were to become collectively known as 'The Scottish Colourists'. Although their careers remained quite independent of each other for considerable periods of time, and progressed in different ways, the four men demonstrated certain shared qualities in their work; the influence of the Glasgow School of Scottish painters that had gone before them, freeing painting from the formal constraints of academic practice, and an appreciation of the use of colour in the work of their contemporaries in France.

In 1905, Peploe obtained a studio in York Place in Edinburgh and in work which he did from that period, the influence of the French painters began to tell. He travelled to France with Fergusson in 1906 to paint, and they both revelled in the strong light that they found there. The colours in Peploe's palette became stronger and sunnier. In 1910, Peploe moved to France and from 1912, worked closely with Fergusson. In that period, the influence of the Cubist painters began to show in Peploe's work; there was a more considered structure and a more schematic quality in his paintings. He returned to Scotland at the outbreak of war and from that period date several of the vibrant and harmonious still lifes for which he is remembered. Although he painted some portraits, including one of himself, owned by the Scottish National Picture Gallery, Peploe concentrated on still life and landscape for most of his career.

PINKERTON, ALLAN
(1819–1884)
Founder of American detective agency

Allan Pinkerton was born in Glasgow. He was a barrel-maker by trade. In 1842 he emigrated to the United States of America and settled in West Dundee, near Chicago, Illinois. There he continued to work as a barrel-maker for the first few years, but in 1846 he was involved in the capture of a gang of counterfeiters and subsequently, he was appointed sheriff of Chicago. He formed Pinkerton's Detective Agency in 1852 and his team successfully investigated a number of train robberies, brought the perpetrators to justice and recovered a large amount of the stolen money. In 1861 the agency scored another major success when a plot to assassinate Abraham Lincoln was foiled at Baltimore. The reputation of the Pinkerton Detective Agency as a formidable force against crime was by then well established and its fame spread far and wide in the United States and across the Atlantic.

During the American Civil War, Pinkerton was put in charge of the secret service, from 1861 to 1862. During the railway strikes in 1877, his detective agency supplied strikebreakers for the government. Pinkerton wrote a number of books during his life, including *Thirty Years a Detective*, published in 1884. He died that same year, aged 65. Pinkerton's sons Robert and William continued to run the detective agency and carry on the work of their formidable father.

RAEBURN, SIR HENRY
(1756–1823)
Portrait painter

Henry Raeburn was born in Edinburgh. He was orphaned at an early age and was educated at George Heriot's Hospital (now George Heriot's School). When he was sixteen, he entered into an apprenticeship with a goldsmith in the city. He taught himself to paint and began by painting miniatures. He then worked for some time in the studio of Edinburgh painter David Martin, who gave him some tuition and helped him to develop his abilities. In spite of his lack of formal training, it was clear that Raeburn was an exceptionally gifted painter. He worked straight onto his canvas with brush and paint, without making any preliminary drawings, or sketches on the canvas itself. He had an uncanny gift of capturing the essence of a sitter's character in his work. His style was vigorous and bold, characterised by broad brushstrokes, with stark contrasts between light and shadow. Evidence can be seen in his work of the influence of Sir Joshua Reynolds, the English portrait painter.

In 1784, Raeburn travelled to Italy – the only time he travelled abroad in his lifetime – and spent some time developing his style further. In 1787, he moved into a studio in Edinburgh's George Street, where, by now widely recognised as the most important portraitist in Scotland, he worked with the brightest, the best and the most aristocratic sitters that Edinburgh society had to offer, including James Boswell, Sir Walter Scott, Niel Gow and David Hume. He was elected ARA in 1812 and RA in 1815. In 1822 he received a knighthood in honour of his work. Among some of the best-known portraits by Raeburn are *The Rev. Robert Walker Skating*, and *MacDonell of Glengarry*.

RAMSAY ALLAN (c.1685–1758)
RAMSAY, ALLAN (1713–84)
POET, PAINTER

Ramsay Senior was born at Leadhills where his father was supervisor of the lead mines. He came to Edinburgh at 14 and became a wig-maker, a lucrative trade in those days, but was far more interested in books and poetry. In 1726 he opened a bookshop and one of the world's first lending libraries – perhaps *the* first. Some of the books offended the more strait-laced members of society (the Kirk still had substantial powers) but Ramsay was a precursor of a more free and easy life-style. He set up a theatre in 1736, promptly shut down by the magistrates, and was a leading spirit of The Easy

Club, a retreat for well-off, literate and convivial types. Ramsay was both a poet and an anthologist; his *Evergreen* and *Tea-Table* collections helped to preserve many poems from earlier times. His eldest son, also Allan Ramsay, trained as a painter, and had a distinguished career in London and Edinburgh, becoming portrait-painter to King George III.

RAMSAY, GORDON JAMES
(1966–)
Chef and Restaurateur

Glasgow-born, the young Ramsay had many homes but the family settled in Stratford-upon-Avon in 1976. He was picked to play football for Warwickshire at 12, but a football career was effectively stopped by a double knee injury in 1984, which ended his chance of playing for Glasgow Rangers. Instead he enrolled in a local college to study catering. Cooking proved to be his true career, satisfying his perfectionism, creativity, managerial abilities, and competitive nature. Moving rapidly upwards in terms of prestigious employments, including almost three years with the tempestuous Marco Pierre White, Ramsay also worked for Albert Roux in London and for Joel Robuchon in Paris: men at the top of the ladder whom he had every intention of emulating. From 1993 to 1997 Ramsay ran the *Aubergine* restaurant in London, then in 1998 opened his own establishment, *Gordon Ramsay at Royal Hospital Road*. By 2001 it had three Michelin stars. Now Gordon Ramsay Holdings operate restaurants in many countries, though not Scotland (his *Amaryllis* in Glasgow had to close) and he has altogether fourteen Michelin stars, a number exceeded by only two other chefs in the world. Notoriously short-tempered, Ramsay's explosive outbursts and obscenities have become his trademark, contributing to his high profile and media appeal across the globe. In 1996 he married Cayetana (Tana) Hutcheson; they have four children.

RANKIN, IAN
(1960–)
Novelist

In traditional novelist's style, Rankin once listed some of his previous occupations: grape picker, swineherd, taxman, alcohol researcher ... Born in Cardenden, Fife, he was a pupil at Beath High School and went on to Edinburgh University. Intending to pursue an academic career in literary studies, he instead opted for the life of a fiction writer. He lived in London for four years and in France for six. In 1987 his first novel featuring the gloomy Edinburgh police detective Rebus was published, and sixteen more have followed – books in which the nature and atmosphere of place is almost as important as the personalities. His crime writing has won awards in the USA, France, Germany and Denmark as well as in Britain, where has also been awarded an OBE. He is a familiar figure in the BBC's *Newsnight* arts coverage and has presented his own TV series on the nature of evil. Rankin lives in Edinburgh with his wife and two sons.

REDPATH, ANNE
(1895–1965)
PAINTER

Anne Redpath was born in Galashiels in the Borders, where her father worked as a designer of textiles. After leaving school, she went to Edinburgh College of Art and in 1917 embarked upon a tour of Belgium, France and Italy, funded by a scholarship. In 1920, after her return to Scotland, she was married to James Michie and they moved to France for fourteen years, during which time she concentrated on bringing up her family and painted comparatively little.

When they returned to Scotland in 1934, they settled in Hawick and Anne began to turn her attentions back to her painting. Her work was very much influenced by the painters of France at the time, whom she much admired, but her knowledge of the work which her father had done also played an important part in her relationship with colour. She held her first solo exhibition in Edinburgh in 1947. From 1948 onwards, she travelled extensively throughout Europe. Her earlier paintings, in particular her still-lifes, demonstrated her absorption with surface pattern and colour and the satisfaction she gained from composing a picture of carefully balanced, bright shapes.

The everyday nature of many of the objects in her still lifes – teacups, tablecloths, slippers – gave a familiar feel to her paintings, while the manner in which they were displayed and painted bestowed on them a quality that was far beyond the everyday and far more joyous. In her later work, her painting, both landscape and still life, became freer and more expressive. She is recognised as a major figure in the Scottish Colourist tradition and one of the most important Scottish artists of the twentieth century. Notable paintings by Anne Redpath include *The Indian Rug*, and *Altar at Chartres*.

REID, JAMES (JIMMY)
(1932–)
SOCIALIST LEADER

Jimmy Reid was born in the slums of Govan. His family was poor and Jimmy's father was often out of work. Jimmy was the sixth of seven children, three of whom died as babies.

Jimmy was bright, and an avid reader, but he left school aged fourteen. He worked as a delivery boy, and in his spare time, read books on the history of the Labour movement and left-wing political theory. He also joined the Labour League of Youth. Then he found a job with a stockbrokers' firm in Glasgow, where he showed considerable promise. He became disenchanted with the Labour Party, resigned and joined the Young Communist League, then realising that his occupation was incompatible with his principles, he left the stockbrokers and began an engineering apprenticeship, ending up at Bristol Polar Engines in Govan. In 1951, he took part in the apprentice's strike and was selected as a delegate for the AEU conference, the beginning of his association with the trade union movement.

In 1952, he was elected National Chairman of the Young Communist League.

In 1953, conscripted for national service, Reid was enrolled in the RAF, where his Communist beliefs caused considerable unease. Then he returned to his former job and became Convenor of Shop Stewards. In 1958, newly married, he became full-time National Secretary of the YCL in London and, in 1959, was elected to the National Executive Committee of the Communist Party. He worked for the party for ten years in England and Scotland then in 1969 he returned to work as a fitter at Upper Clyde Shipbuilders (UCS). He kept up his commitment to the Communist Party, serving on the NEC and the PC, and was also elected as a councillor in Clydebank, as Convenor of the Amalgamated Engineering Unions and Chairman of the Outfit Trades.

In 1971 Edward Heath's government commissioned a report on UCS, recommending liquidation and the loss of 70 percent of jobs. The response of the workers, led by Reid, was a work-in, combined with a publicity campaign. Reid's revelations about the government's tactics to enforce liquidation brought mass support to their cause and the government was forced to admit defeat. Three yards received further funding, one was sold off with a financial support package. No jobs were lost.

Between 1971 and 1974, Reid was Rector of Glasgow University. During the 1970s, while remaining totally committed to his Socialist beliefs, he became increasingly distanced from the Communist Party. Finally, unable to reconcile his principles with the political machinery within a party which he considered to be stagnating, he resigned in 1976.

Reid supported Labour up until the 1997 election when he became disillusioned with its movement to New Labour. He has since been a supporter of Scottish nationalism and independence for Scotland and Wales. He joined the SNP in 2005.

REITH, JOHN CHARLES WALSHAM, 1ST BARON OF STONEHAVEN
(1889–1971)
DIRECTOR GENERAL OF THE BBC

John Reith was born in Stonehaven. His father was a minister. He was educated in Glasgow, but did not go to university. Instead, he served an apprenticeship as an engineer. He was wounded while serving in the First World War, and worked in munitions supply from 1916 until the end of the war. After the war he worked as a manager for engineering giants William Beardmore and Co.

Then in 1922, he was appointed as General Manager of the British Broadcasting Company, at that time a private company, still in its infancy. He was very committed to his job. His belief was that broadcasting should be a public service and should not merely entertain, but also encompass a wide range of other interests, from culture and religion to politics, educating and informing viewers rather than simply catering for more trivial tastes for the sake of commercial appeal. Reith was a strong leader and had risen to become Director General by 1927. During his time at the BBC, radio became a public service and regular television transmissions had begun.

In 1938, Reith left the BBC and took on the position of chairman of Imperial Airways, which was merged with British Airways to become BOAC. In the same year, he was elected MP for Southampton and in 1940, became Minister for Works and Buildings. Conflict with Winston Churchill led to his dismissal from the wartime cabinet in 1942, and he became a lieutenant commander in the Royal Naval Volunteer Reserve. After the war, he served in a variety of executive posts, and was chairman of the Telecommunications Board from 1946 to 1950.

Reith was by all accounts a strong character, feared by some, adored by others, but respected by most of those who came into contact with him. He lived his own life according to strict Presbyterian rules and did not suffer fools gladly. His greatest achievement was, undoubtedly, building the foundations of public service broadcasting in Great Britain. He died in Edinburgh in June, 1971.

ROB ROY (ROBERT MacGREGOR)
(1671–1734)
OUTLAW AND FOLK HERO

Rob Roy (meaning 'Red Robert' in Gaelic) was born in Buchanan, Stirlingshire. A Jacobite, he was a skilled swordsman and fought on the side of Bonnie Dundee at the Battle of Killiecrankie in 1689. For some time he lived as a cattle dealer and became quite wealthy, owning property on Loch Lomondside and at Balquidder. In 1712, some of his men deserted him, taking with them money owed to the Duke of Montrose. Montrose seized Rob Roy's lands in retaliation and had him declared an outlaw. Rob Roy then turned to a life of cattle and sheep theft and extorted money from wealthy owners by blackmail (payment in exchange for protection). His exploits in the area around the Trossachs became legend and he became something of a folk hero as in the coming years he continued to avoid imprisonment in spite of all attempts to bring him to justice (some of which came perilously close to success). He gathered a force of his clan to fight for the Jacobites in 1715, and in 1716 was given protection by the Duke of Argyll. He was finally arrested in 1727 and narrowly escaped transportation when he was given the King's pardon. He spent his last years peacefully and died in 1734. His life story was used as the basis for SIR WALTER SCOTT's historical novel, *Rob Roy*, published in 1818.

SALMOND, ALEXANDER ELLIOT ANDERSON (ALEX)
(1954–)
POLITICIAN

Assured of his place in history as leader of Scotland's first National Party government, Salmond is a powerful and effective political heavyweight. Born in Linlithgow, the son of civil servants, he attended Linlithgow Academy and then read Economics and History at the University of St Andrews. First employed in the Department of Agriculture and Fisheries, he moved in 1980 to the Royal Bank of Scotland where he stayed until his election in 1987 as SNP Member of Parliament for Banff and Buchan.

His involvement with nationalist politics had begun as a student and he was strongly identified with a socialist-republican element, the 79 Group, within the National Party. As he rose within the party hierarchy, his views became more middle-of-the-road. He has been party leader twice, from 1990–2000 and again from 2004. A member of Scotland's first modern parliament in 1999, he left it in 2001 to lead the SNP group in the House of Commons, and returned to it in 2007, having led the SNP to its one-seat victory over Labour. Since then he has shown political dexterity in running a minority government.

Salmond married Moira McGlashan in 1981.

SCOTT, SIR WALTER
(1771–1832)
LAWYER, POET, NOVELIST AND CRITIC

Walter Scott, was the son of an Edinburgh lawyer, also named Walter. After contracting polio in his second year, he spent much of his early childhood on his grandfather's farm at Sandyknowe, near Kelso and then returned to Edinburgh where he attended the High School, completing his education at Edinburgh University. After working for his father for some time, he studied for the Bar and was admitted to the Faculty of Advocates in 1792. His first love, however, was literature, and in spite of performing his legal duties diligently, he took care to ensure that they permitted him enough free time in which to write.

A love of traditional songs and ballads which had begun in his childhood years in the Borders steered his writing. In 1796, his first publication came out; a rhyming translation of German ballads by Gottfried Bürger. This was followed by a translation of Goethe's *Göetz von Berlichingen* in 1799, and then his first collection of Scottish ballads, *The Minstrelsy of the Scottish Border*, was published in three volumes, between 1802 and 1803. This work, and his narrative poem 'The Lay of the Last Minstrel' (1805), made him a very popular writer. A string of narrative poems followed from this success, including 'Marmion' (1808), 'The Lady of the Lake' (1810), 'Rokeby' (1813) and 'The Lord of the Isles' (1815). He also edited *The Life and Works of John Dryden* and *The Life and Works of Jonathan Swift*. Over time, Scott began to feel that his popularity as a poet was dropping and he turned his creative pen to the novel. In 1814, his first historical novel, *Waverley*, was published and was an immediate success. Scott wrote more than twenty books of this nature in total, the most famous including *Guy Mannering* (1815), *The Heart of Midlothian* (1818), *Rob Roy* (1817), *Ivanhoe* (1820) and *Kenilworth* (1821). He published the novels anonymously and used the money he earned to start building an extravagant house at Abbotsford for himself, his wife, Charlotte

Charpentier, whom he married in 1797, and their four children. But in 1826 financial problems loomed when the printing firm Scott had set up with James and John Ballantyne and the publishers with which he was associated, Constable and Co., ran into difficulties. Scott was declared bankrupt and was left with a mountain of debt. With the express intention of paying off his creditors, he published *The Life of Napoleon*, four more fictional works and a set of new revised editions of his novels, *The Waverley Novels*, under his own name, with additional notes. He worked himself into the ground but managed to pay off a significant portion of his debt. His health then began to decline rapidly. He travelled abroad to try to recuperate between 1831 and 1832 but died at Abbotsford in September 1832.

ALEXANDER SELKIRK
(1676–1721)
Sailor

Alexander Selkirk, or Selcraig, was born in the little town of Largo on the east coast of Fife. His father was a shoemaker by trade but Alexander, who was rather a wild lad by all accounts, did not follow him into the business. He opted for a life of adventure and ran away to sea when he was in his late teens. In 1704, aged twenty-seven, he joined the services of explorer and adventurer turned buccaneer, Captain William Dampler, but the two men found themselves at loggerheads while sailing in the Pacific and Selkirk rashly requested that the captain put him ashore. He was left on an island called

Juan Fernandez, which was completely uninhabited. Against all odds he survived there alone for nearly four and a half years, until he was finally rescued by another vessel in 1709. He eventually returned to his home town in 1712 with an amazing story to tell. The account of Selkirk's experiences during his solitary spell on Juan Fernandez provided the writer Daniel Defoe with the material to write his famous novel *Robinson Crusoe*, which was published in 1719. Selkirk did not settle in Largo; he returned instead to the seafaring life and was serving as a lieutenant on a Royal Navy man o' war when he died in 1721.

SHANKLY, BILL
(1913–1981)
FOOTBALL PLAYER AND MANAGER

Bill Shankly is remembered with fond affection and great respect by all those involved in the footballing professions in Great Britain. He was born in Glenbuck, a mining village in Ayrshire. He began his career in football with a signing as a player for Carlisle United in 1932. He then transferred to Preston North End. During his playing career he was capped seven times for Scotland, but the Second World War intervened. When the war was over, Shankly made the decision to move into football management. He began working with Carlisle United, then moved on to Grimsby, Workington and Huddersfield in turn, but he met with little success in these posts. Then in 1959 he was given the job of manager of Liverpool, the position in which he was to make his name as one of football's greatest. When Shankly took over at Liverpool, the club was in a poor state and the team was in the second division. However Shankly's commitment to his men, his conviction in his training methods and his sheer dedication to and enthusiasm for the game gradually began to pay off. Liverpool's successes began to rise in number and as the standard of football offered by the team improved, so the support from the fans grew. In the 1963–64 season, with Liverpool back in the first division, Everton were knocked from their pedestal as league champions. The team went from strength to strength in Britain and in Europe during the 1960s and early 1970s, and in 1973, Shankly led them to victory in the UEFA cup. Shankly retired from his post on a high note in 1974, aged 60. His years of retiral were tragically cut short when he died suddenly from a heart attack in 1981. His death was mourned by the football fraternity throughout the country.

SIM, ALASTAIR
(1900–1976)
ACTOR

Alastair Sim was born in Edinburgh, where his father had a tailoring business. He was interested in the theatre from an early age. After a period as a lecturer in elocution at Edinburgh University, Alastair took up acting as a professional. His professional stage debut was in 1930, when he appeared in a production of *Othello* in London. Although he continued to work on stage throughout his career, appearing in both dramatic and comic roles, he diversified into films in 1935, when he first appeared on screen in *Riverside Murder*. His film career saw him acting in a wide variety of roles in which his gift as a character actor of enormous versatility could be exploited to the full. He starred in some fifty films between 1930 and 1976, including *Green for Danger* (1946), *Inspector Hornleigh* (1939) (the first of three Inspector Hornleigh films), *The Happiest Days of Your Life* (1950), *Laughter in Paradise* (1951), *Scrooge* (1951), *An Inspector Calls* (1954), *The Belles of St Trinian's* (1954), *The Green Man* (1956), *Blue Murder at St Trinian's* (1957), and *The Ruling Class* (1972). For many people, the most memorable film in which he appeared is *The Belles of St Trinian's*, in which he played a double role as the headmistress of St Trinian's and her brother, to hilarious effect.

Alastair Sim worked as an actor right up until his death in 1976.

SIMPSON, SIR JAMES YOUNG
(1811–1870)
OBSTETRICIAN, PIONEER OF ANAESTHESIA

James Simpson was born in Bathgate. At the age of fourteen, he began his studies at Edinburgh University and two years later took up medicine. He qualified as a doctor in 1832 and chose obstetrics as a speciality. In 1835, he was appointed Professor of Midwifery. Driven to find something that would safely and effectively ease the pain of a difficult childbirth, he pioneered the use of ether in 1847. In the same year, he investigated the potential of chloroform as an anaesthetic, taking the unusual and risky step of experimenting on himself. Despite objections by the church on moral grounds and by the medical profession on physical grounds, Simpson campaigned persistently for the use of chloroform with increasing success.

When he was appointed as a physician to Queen Victoria and she permitted the use of chloroform during the birth of her son Leopold, Simpson knew that his critics would be silenced at last. Simpson did a great deal to improve services to women in gynaecology and obstetrics and in 1866 he was made a baronet in recognition of his work.

When he died he was buried at Warriston cemetery in Edinburgh. A statue of James Simpson stands in the city's Princes Street Gardens and his house in Queen Street is marked with a plaque. The city's maternity hospital built in the grounds of the old Royal Infirmary of Edinburgh was named The Simpson Memorial Maternity Pavilion in his honour.

SLESSOR, MARY
(1848–1915)
MISSIONARY

Mary Slessor was born in Aberdeen and was no stranger to hardship in her childhood and early adulthood. Her father, a shoemaker by trade, was a heavy drinker and the family were poor. When Mary was nine years old, her family moved to Dundee and it was not long before

Mary found herself shouldering adult responsibilities. By the age of eleven, she was working in a jute mill in the city. Three years after this, her father died. Her mother kept poor health and her two older brothers had both died young. As the eldest of three remaining girls, Mary became responsible for caring for the family until her sisters were both of an age to work for themselves.

Mary took up her calling as a missionary of the United Presbyterian Church in 1875, and in 1876 was given a posting in West Africa, in Calabar, Nigeria. Her own attitude to her calling was at variance with those held at the mission and she opted to strike out on her own in a remote area further inland where no white men had yet ventured.

There, undaunted by the fact that she was very isolated and vulnerable, she adopted a simple manner of dress and a lifestyle which suited her better to her surroundings and to the people she lived with. She ate the same foods as the local people did and studied their native customs, traditions and language in depth. She endeared herself greatly to the people amongst whom she lived and won not only their affection but also their respect, becoming known in time as the 'Great Mother' or 'Ma'. Many orphaned or abandoned babies became part of the large adopted family of Mary Slessor.

Mary stayed in Calabar for the rest of her life, living as a leader in her community in Okyon district. Those whom she guided and cared for returned her affection by caring for her through several periods of illness, in particular, malaria, over the years. Eventually, however, ill health wore her down and she died from malaria and dysentery in 1915, aged 67.

SMITH, ADAM
(1723–1790)
Economist

Adam Smith was born in Kirkcaldy in Fife. He was educated at the universities of Glasgow and Oxford. In 1746 he returned to Scotland from Oxford and gave a series of lectures on rhetoric in Edinburgh. During this period he became friends with the philosopher David Hume. In 1752, he was elected Professor of Moral Philosophy at Glasgow University and in 1759, he published a series of the lectures he had given in Glasgow in *The Theory of Moral Sentiments*. In 1763, Smith resigned his post to take up an appointment as tutor to the sons of the Duke of Buccleuch and while travelling with them made the acquaintance of other great thinkers including Quesnay, Robert and Turgot who, as Hume had done before, shaped and influenced his ideas.

In 1766 Smith returned to Kirkcaldy and spent the next ten years compiling his major work, *An Inquiry into the Nature and Causes of the Wealth of Nations*, a masterpiece of political, economic and philosophical thought. In the same year, he published a moving account of the death of his friend David Hume, which caused quite a scandal. Hume had been an atheist, a factor which had prevented him from achieving academic positions as a philosopher, and the idea of his peaceful and serene departure from life was at odds with religious beliefs of the time.

The Wealth of Nations has formed the basis for the study of economics in universities and colleges all over Europe and some of his theories, in spite of social and political change over the years, still underpin many of the ideas of those involved in economics and politics in modern times.

In 1778, Smith was appointed Commissioner of Customs in Edinburgh. He died in Edinburgh in 1790 and was buried in the Canongate churchyard.

SMITH, JOHN
(1938–1994)
LABOUR POLITICIAN

John Smith was born in the west of Scotland. He was a pupil at Dunoon Grammar School before going to Glasgow University, where he studied for a career in law. He studied for the Bar and became an advocate in 1967. A love of debating and a natural gift for public speaking led to his taking first prize in the *Observer* Mace debating competition in 1962. In 1970 he stood as Labour candidate for Lanarkshire North and was elected as MP. He served in the Wilson administration from 1974 to 1976, then Callaghan became leader from 1976 to 1979, and Smith was appointed Trade Secretary in 1978. Following Labour's defeat in 1979, Smith served as opposition Front Bench Spokesman on Trade, Energy, Employment and Economic affairs. In 1988, he suffered a major heart attack and it was feared that his career as a politician might be over. However, he recovered and returned with renewed vigour in 1989. The 'Thatcher Years' were drawing to a close by this time and the Labour Party was hopeful of a return to strength and to power.

After the disappointment of defeat in the general election of 1992, Neil Kinnock resigned as leader of the opposition and John Smith took his place. The party increased in strength still further under his leadership and partly because of this, and partly because of the fall in support for the Conservative Party, it was widely believed that John Smith would lead Labour to victory and become Prime Minister at the next general election.

This belief was given added conviction when the Conservative Party suffered devastating losses to Labour in the 1994 local elections. Had he lived, there can be little doubt that John Smith would have been a popular premier. In his last speech to Labour supporters in London in May 1994, he stressed the hopes of his party: 'A chance to serve; that is all we ask.'

Very soon afterwards, he suffered another heart attack and died. The friendship and deep respect which politicians of all parties had felt for Smith was very much in evidence in parliament on the day his death was announced, and later, at his funeral in Edinburgh. He was buried on the island of Iona.

SPARK, DAME MURIEL
(1918–2006)
Poet, biographer and novelist

Muriel Spark was born in Edinburgh. Her father was an engineer and her mother was a suffragette. She attended James Gillespie's High School for Girls in Edinburgh and continued her studies at the Heriot Watt College. When she was twenty, she married and went to live in Central Africa for some years. The marriage was unhappy and her husband was violent. She separated from her husband and returned to Great Britain in the 1940s where she obtained a post working in the Foreign Office, in Intelligence. She had had a love of writing and of poetry since her schooldays, and from 1947 to 1949 she was editor of the *Poetry Review*. Eventually she devoted herself full time to her writing.

The main body of her work in the early 1950s was nonfiction; she wrote biographical works on Wordsworth, Mary Shelley, Emily Bronte and John Masefield. But it is as a novelist that Muriel Spark has become famous. Her reputation was established with her early novels, including *The Comforters* (1957), *Memento Mori* (1959) and *The Ballad of Peckham Rye* (1960). Then in 1961, her best known work, *The Prime of Miss Jean Brodie* was published. Set in the period leading up to the Second World War, it is the story of an idiosyncratic, domineering and progressive-thinking teacher at a girl's school in Edinburgh, and the group of girls whom she has selected from among her pupils to guide and nurture. A witty and perceptive sketch of life in a 'nice' Edinburgh girls' school, the tale nevertheless has a darker and more disturbing aspect revealed in the effect which Miss Brodie has on her girls' lives and vice versa. Several other successful and exceptional novels followed, including *Girls of Slender Means* (1963), *The Mandelbaum Gate* (1965) *The Abbess of Crewe* (1974), *Loitering With Intent* (1981), *The Only Problem* (1984), and *A Far Cry from Kensington* (1988); two collections of short stories have also been published. In her latter years she produced *Symposium* (1991), *Reality and Dreams* (1996), *Aiding and Abetting*, and *The Finishing School* (2004). Several of Spark's novel's have been adapted for film and stage, and *Doctors of Philosophy* (1962) was written specifically for theatre.

During most of this time, Muriel Spark lived abroad. She was awarded an OBE in 1967, was made a Dame of the British Empire in 1993 and has been awarded honorary degrees from the Universities of Edinburgh and Strathclyde. The first volume of her autobiography was published in 1992.

She died in April of 2006 in Tuscany, where she had lived with her friend Penelope Jardine since the 70s, aged 88.

STEIN, JOHN (JOCK)
(1922–1985)
FOOTBALL MANAGER

Jock Stein was born in Burnbank, Lanarkshire. After an undistinguished career as a footballer he found his true vocation as a manager. His first post was at Dunfermline Athletic where he led the team to victory in the Scottish Cup. He then moved to Hibernian for a short spell before he was offered the post of manager at Glasgow Celtic, a club he had played for in previous years. He started work with the club in 1965 and in the thirteen years in which Jock Stein was in charge, Celtic won a string of trophies, including the League Cup, Scottish Cup and Scottish Championship victories. His greatest triumph as manager of Celtic was when his team won the European Cup in Lisbon in 1967 and in 1970. A repeat was narrowly missed when the team became finalists for a second time. In 1978, Stein left Celtic and went to Leeds United for a brief period, but returned to Scotland to take charge of the national squad. Under his guidance, the Scottish team qualified for the World Cup finals in 1982. He was still active with the Scottish squad when he died during a game between Scotland and Wales at Cardiff. Along with BUSBY, SHANKLY and FERGUSON, Jock Stein ranks among the finest managers the game of football has known.

STEVENSON, ROBERT
(1772–1850)
LIGHTHOUSE ENGINEER

Robert Stevenson was born in Glasgow. His father, a merchant, died when he was two years old. In 1791, Stevenson began working as an apprentice under a lampmaker and engineer, who was the Engineer of the Northern Lighthouse Board, Thomas Smith. Stevenson was fascinated by the field of engineering and took on additional studies at Glasgow University. In the late 1790s Stevenson took over from Smith as Engineer of the Lighthouse Board, became a partner in Smith's firm, and married Smith's daughter Jane. Smith had married Stevenson's mother some years earlier.

In his capacity as a lighthouse engineer, Stevenson was responsible for the planning and construction of more than twenty lighthouses. His designs for the lighting systems in some of these structures were innovative and ingenious and it was Stevenson who invented the system of a revolving, flashing light to make the beam from the lighthouse easily distinguishable. The Bell Rock lighthouse is perhaps the best-known of the lighthouses built by Stevenson.

Stevenson's engineering skills were also applied to other fields and he was consulted on the construction of roads, canals and bridges all over Scotland. He worked on the plans to drain the Nor' Loch, now Princes Street Gardens, in Edinburgh and he took an active interest in the railways, both in the construction of the locomotives and rails, and in the planning for rail routes. Stevenson's sons, Alan, David and Thomas, all joined their father's business and continued building lighthouses and undertaking a variety of engineering projects after his death.

STEVENSON, ROBERT LOUIS BALFOUR

(1850–1894)

WRITER

Robert Louis Stevenson was born in Edinburgh on November 13th, 1850. His father, Thomas, was a lighthouse engineer. Stevenson was educated at Edinburgh Academy for a brief period, but he kept very poor health as a child and the family travelled abroad a great deal in an effort to alleviate his chronic lung problems. Stevenson studied engineering and then law at Edinburgh University but he felt a pull towards writing. His travels in France and Belgium after he left university provided the subject-matter for two of his first books, *An Inland Voyage*, published in 1878, and *Travels with a Donkey in the Cevènnes*, published in 1879.

While he was in France he met an American divorcee, Frances Osbourne. He followed her to California and married her in 1880. His time in America resulted in another book, *The Silverado Squatters*.

On his return to Europe his ill-health did not improve, but he wrote prolifically. He moved from travel writing into fiction, publishing short stories in various magazines. *Treasure Island*, one of his best-known books, was published in 1883 and *Kidnapped*, another timeless favourite, was published in 1886. *Strange Case of Dr Jekyll and Mr Hyde*, published in 1886, was quite different from adventure stories such as these; it was more of a psychological thriller, exploring the darker side of man. Then followed *The Black Arrow* and *The Master of Ballantrae* in 1889, and *Catriona* in 1893. His last novels, *Weir of Hermiston* and *St Ives* were left unfinished at his death. Stevenson wrote a number of plays, including *Deacon Brodie* and *Admiral Guinea*, which were written in collaboration with William Henley, the poet, in 1880 and 1884 respectively. He also wrote poetry and published collections of verse including *Underwoods* (1887), *Ballads* (1890) and *Songs of Travel* (1895). His recollections of childhood, gathered together in *A Child's Garden of Verses*, remain popular with children and their parents alike today.

Stevenson's ill-health continued to wear him down constantly and he and his wife emigrated to Samoa in 1888, in an attempt to find a climate in which he might recover some of his vitality. He spent his last years there and died in December 1894.

STEWART, PRINCE CHARLES EDWARD
(1720–1788)
'The Young Pretender' or 'Bonnie Prince Charlie', claimant to the throne of Scotland and England

Charles Edward Stewart was the grandson of James VII and II, and the son of James Francis Stewart, or 'The Old Pretender'. He was born and brought up in Rome. He was a well-educated and charismatic young man and determined to reclaim the throne that his grandfather had lost to William of Orange.

In 1744, he went to France to raise support for an

invasion of England but storms and the threat to the French from the British fleet caused havoc to his plans and when he finally reached British shores, landing at Moidart in 1745, he had but a handful of followers. Charles raised the Jacobite standard at Glenfinnan in August that year and several highland chiefs pledged their support to him. He marched with his supporters to Edinburgh, where they captured the city, but failed to gain control of the castle. In September, after defeating the forces of Sir John Cope at the Battle of Prestonpans, he marched southwards, hoping to gather additional support for his cause on the way to London. After taking Carlisle, the Jacobite force got as far as Derby, when it became clear that the English Catholics would not offer the support that had been hoped for.

The army turned back northwards and although they won another battle at Falkirk, their force was weakened by months of marching in the bitter winter weather, and reduced in numbers after the withdrawal of many of the highlanders. They suffered a crushing defeat at Culloden against the Duke of Cumberland in April 1746 and Charles was forced to flee. After five months as a fugitive in the highlands, he was smuggled to Skye with the help of Flora Macdonald, and from there escaped to France. He was expelled from France in 1748 after the Treaty of Aix-la-Chappelle and moved around Europe for some years before finally settling in Italy in 1766.

The promising young Jacobite leader had now become a much less attractive middle-aged man, over-fond of alcohol and prone to fits of temper and violence. He was married in 1772 to Louisa, Duchess of Albany, but the marriage was a failure and she deserted him eight years later. On the first of two secret visits to London in 1750 and 1754, he had taken Clementina Walkinshaw as a mistress. She had a daughter by him, named Charlotte, whom Charles created Duchess of Albany and took to live with him in Italy. Charles died in Rome, where he was buried.

STEWART, JOHN YOUNG (JACKIE)
(1939–)
MOTOR-RACING DRIVER

Jackie Stewart was born in Dumbartonshire in June 1939. He came from a motor-racing family; his father was a former motorcycle racer and his brother Jimmy was also involved in the sport. Jackie's parents were not anxious to have another family member risking life and limb on the race track and did their best to encourage their son's interests in other directions. He was a keen target shooter and came close to shooting at Olympic standard, but the motor-racing bug finally caught him when he was offered the chance of testing cars at a racetrack close to home and discovered that not only did he love the thrill of high-speed driving, but he also had a natural aptitude for it. In 1963 he joined the Cooper Formula junior team under Ken Tyrell. In 1965, he made his debut in Formula One racing with BRM and won the Italian Grand Prix at Monza. He rose to fame as a top world-class racing driver in 1968, when, driving for Tyrell's team, he won three Grand Prix races, in the Netherlands, Germany and the USA. He built on these successes and went on to become World Champion three times in the next five years, in 1969, 1970, 1973. In addition to his three world championships, Stewart won a total of twenty seven Grand Prix races during his driving career. His nickname, 'The Flying Scot', is well-deserved.

After his victory in 1973, he made the decision to retire from Formula One racing as a driver, but maintained an active interest in the sport, campaigning for improved safety standards on the racetracks and giving television commentaries of racing events. He and his son Paul owned their own team, Stewart Grand Prix. In 2000 the team was sold to the Ford Motor Company.

Jackie Stewart was knighted in the Queen's birthday honours list in 2001. He is a founding patron of the Scottish Sports Hall of Fame, and was an inaugural inductee in 2002.

In November 2008 Stewart was awarded an honorary Doctor of Science degree from the University of St Andrews.

SWINTON, KATHERINE MATILDA (TILDA)
(1960–)
ACTRESS

Always notable for imaginative projects and roles, Tilda Swinton was born in Dunfermline, her mother Australian and her father an army general descended from an old Border family. After West Heath Girls'

School, in Kent, and a short time at Fettes College, Edinburgh, she went to Cambridge University and graduated in Social and Political Science. The stage called her, however, and she worked with the Traverse Theatre in Edinburgh, and the Royal Shakespeare Company, before moving into film in the mid-1980s. Her early films were of the art-house sort, and she also experimented with installation art, herself being part of the display. Since around 2000, she has been seen in more mainstream films, culminating in her Oscar and BAFTA award as 'Best Supporting Actress' in *Michael Clayton*. Swinton's home is in Nairn, with her long-standing partner John Byrne, with whom she has had twin sons. In recent years she has also formed a parallel relationship with the painter Sandro Kopp.

TELFORD, THOMAS
(1757–1834)
ENGINEER

Thomas Telford was born in Westerkirk, Langholm, in Dumfriesshire. When he was fourteen years old, he was apprenticed to a stonemason and after he had finished his apprenticeship he worked in Edinburgh for a period before moving to London in 1782. He studied the principles of architecture independently and took a supervisory role in the construction of various public buildings. He was then appointed as Surveyor of Public Works in Shropshire in 1788. In this position he was responsible, among other things, for the work on the Ellesmere Canal, which involved the construction of nineteen locks and two impressive aqueducts at Chirk and Pont-y-Cysylltau. The project lasted from 1793 to 1805 and won Telford great acclaim when it was completed.

His reputation as a surveyor, architect and engineer having thus been established, Telford was then appointed in 1802 to carry out a survey of communications in the highlands of Scotland and to implement the proposals stemming from his findings. Thus, in the following years, he was responsible for the construction of the Caledonian Canal between 1803 and 1847, for the building of more than nine hundred miles of new roads and for the construction of 1200 bridges, as well as a large number of public buildings and several harbours.

Telford worked at a tremendous rate and in addition to the enormous task he completed in Scotland, he was involved in a great number of other road, bridge and canal projects in England and Wales. He also built the Gotha Canal in Sweden. Apart from the Caledonian Canal, some of his most notable works include the road from London to Holyhead, the Menai Bridge, the bridge over the Tay at Dunkeld, the Dean Bridge in Edinburgh and St Katherine's Dock in London. His structures stand as monuments of his skill and energy all over the country.

When Telford died in 1834 he was buried in Westminster Abbey.

THOMSON, SIR WILLIAM, LORD KELVIN
(1824–1907)
SCIENTIST, MATHEMATICIAN

William Thomson was born in Belfast and moved to Glasgow when his father was appointed Professor of Mathematics at the university there. William entered the university himself at the age of eleven and progressed to Peterhouse College, Cambridge in 1841. After a further period of study in Paris, he returned to Glasgow and was appointed Professor of Mathematics and Natural Philosophy in 1846.

Thomson proved himself a brilliant scientist in both theoretical and practical work. In 1848, he proposed an absolute scale of temperature, the Kelvin scale, and along with Clausius, he established the second law of thermodynamics. He studied and made valuable contributions to work on hydrodynamics, geomagnetism, electrostatics and wave dynamics amongst other things and published several hundred papers on his work.

His love of applied science was manifest in his many inventions. He patented more than fifty of these, including a marine compass, the mirror galvanometer, navigational aids and numerous electrical devices, and he set up a company to manufacture his designs. His invention of the mirror galvanometer and his work on the development of insulated telegraph cable contributed considerably to the progress of telegraphic communications, and he was consultant and supervisor when the first submarine electric cable was laid across the Atlantic, from Ireland to Newfoundland.

Thomson received many honours in recognition of his work as a teacher and a scientist during his lifetime. He became a Fellow of the Royal Society in 1851, and served as president from 1890 to 1895. He was made Baron Kelvin of Largs in 1892, and Chancellor of Glasgow University in 1904. When he died, he was buried in Westminster Abbey.

TRANTER, NIGEL
(1909–2000)
Novelist and Architectural Historian

Nigel Tranter was born in Glasgow but the family moved to Edinburgh and he was educated at George Heriot's School. As a teenager he developed a lifelong interest in architecture and particularly in the fortified buildings of Scotland. After school he joined an architectural practice but when his father died, financial pressures forced him to transfer to an insurance company run by an uncle. His first book appeared in 1934, on *The Forticles and Early Mansions of Southern Scotland*, but his wife May (they married in 1933) also encouraged him to write fiction. In the Second World War he served in the Royal Artillery but continued to write. His early fiction was very much of the pot-boiler type, swiftly-written romances with a Scottish background, but also Westerns. From the 1950s, he embarked on novels with a richer and more researched historical content, covering virtually all the major characters of Scottish history. His *Robert the Bruce* trilogy (1969–71) is perhaps his best achievement in the genre. At the same time he was compiling and illustrating the five-volume *Fortified House in Scotland* and new editions of the 'Queen's Scotland' regional topographies.

VETTRIANO, JACK
(1951–)
PAINTER

Born Jack Hoggan in Methil, Fife, he left school at 16 and at first seemed intended for a career in engineering. Given a set of watercolour paints for his 21st birthday present, he began to paint, and found it a satisfying hobby. He never attended art school. In 1988 after 14 years of spare-time painting, he submitted two canvases to the Royal Scottish Academy's annual show. Both were accepted, and sold on the first day; and the artist was approached by several galleries keen to show more of his work. He moved to Edinburgh, adopting his mother's maiden name of Vettrino but adding an 'a'. His marriage broke down at this time, but commercial success transformed his life. Before long he had an international reputation and clientèle. What was to elude him was praise and acceptance by the art establishment. His paintings have been criticised as slick and derivative, but their appeal to a wide public is incontestable. His famous seaside scene, *The Singing Butler*, is the most-reproduced picture in the UK.

Vettriano maintains studios in Scotland and in London, and was awarded an OBE in 2003.

WALLACE, SIR WILLIAM
(c. 1274–1305)
Scottish hero

Little is known about the early life of William Wallace, but he is believed to have been born in Elderslie, near Paisley. This is according to Henry the Minstrel, or Blind Harry, a fifteenth century poet whose work, although widely criticised as inaccurate by historians, is a source of much of the biographical information on Wallace. His struggles against the English during the War of Independence began with the death of an English Sheriff at Lanark in 1297. Outlawed by the English, he burnt the garrison at Lanark and went on to defeat English Forces of Edward I, 'Hammer of the Scots', at the Battle of Stirling Bridge later that same year. In November 1297, he was elected Guardian of Scotland after having driven the English back from Berwick and carried out a number of successful raids south of the border. He was knighted at Ettrick in 1298.

Edward's forces returned to Scotland in 1298 to seek revenge upon the Scots and marched northward to meet Wallace's troops at Falkirk. Wallace suffered defeat and was forced to flee. He resigned his Guardianship of Scotland and sought refuge in France in 1299 where he remained for some time, trying to muster support for his cause. By the time he returned to Scotland in 1303, he had been declared an outlaw and his position had weakened considerably. The support of the Scottish nobles was dwindling and more of them were beginning to show willing to accept the rule of Edward. Wallace was betrayed to the enemy and in 1305 was taken prisoner at Robroyston by Sir John Menteith, the Sheriff of Dumbarton. Menteith brought Wallace to London where he was tried at Westminster on a charge of treason. He was condemned to death, hanged, drawn and quartered, and his quarters were despatched to Newcastle, Berwick, Stirling and Perth to be displayed as a warning to the Scots rebels. William Wallace is remembered as the greatest champion of the Scots in their struggle for independence. The Oscar-winning film *Braveheart* follows Blind Harry's story of Wallace's life.

WATSON-WATT, SIR ROBERT ALEXANDER
(1892–1973)
SCIENTIST, INVENTOR OF RADAR

Robert Watson-Watt was born in Brechin, Angus. He attended Dundee University and the University of St Andrews. After completing his education he worked for the British government carrying out research in the meteorological office. He then moved to the Department of Scientific and Industrial Research and then to the National Physical Laboratory. In the course of his work, he carried out extensive studies into radio waves and after the First World War, became particularly interested in the application of his studies to the field of aviation. His first patent for a radar device was obtained in 1919, and in 1935 he finally managed to construct a short wave device that was capable of locating aircraft by night or day at distances of over one hundred miles. The development of the system, Radio Detection And Ranging, was very timely, for it meant that in the years to come, in the Second World War, Britain was equipped with an effective early warning and defence system against enemy aircraft. The radar defence system was set up under the supervision of Watson-Watt, who became Scientific Adviser to the Air Ministry in 1940 and contributed in a large part to victory in the Battle of Britain.

Watson-Watt received a knighthood for his work in 1942 and was also awarded the United States Medal for Merit in 1946.

He wrote a number of books during his career, including *Through the Weather House* (1935), *Three Steps to Victory* (1958), *The Pulse of Radar* (1959), and *Man's Means to his End* (1961). He died in Inverness in 1973.

WATT, ALISON
(1965–)
PAINTER

Alison Watt was born in Greenock and graduated from Glasgow School of Art in 1988. While still a student, she won the John Player Portrait Award and as a result was commissioned to paint a portrait of the Queen Mother. Her best-known early works, however, were dryly painted figurative canvases, often female nudes, in brightly-lit interiors. She became increasingly interested in depicting fabrics in her canvases, picking up on something that several 19th century French painters, including Ingres, had also been stimulated by. In 2000 she became the youngest artist to have a solo exhibition at the Scottish National Gallery of Modern Art, with *Shift,* in which twelve huge paintings featured fabric alone. From January 2006 to February 2008, she was artist in residence at the National Gallery, London. She was appointed OBE in the 2008 New Year Honours.

WATT, JAMES
(1736–1819)
Scientist, engineer

James Watt was born in Greenock, where he attended the local grammar school. An aptitude for mathematics led to his apprenticeship as a scientific instrument maker and in 1757 he was employed by the University of Glasgow in this capacity, remaining there until 1763. In 1763 a model of Thomas Newcomen's steam engine was brought to Watt for repair, and while carrying out the repairs, Watt began to realise that improvements could be made to its efficiency. Two years later, after conducting some experiments in his own time on the nature of steam and latent heat, Watt came up with the idea of condensing the steam not in the working cylinder, but in a separate condenser.

Watt was hindered in his attempts to develop this idea because of lack of finance. The financial support of Professor Joseph Black and Dr John Roebuck was not enough to carry his work through to completion. A patent was obtained in 1769 for his engine, but he had not the means to put it into production. From 1766 to 1774, he worked in civil engineering, amongst other things conducting surveys for the Forth and Clyde Canal, the Crinan Canal and the Monkland Canal. Then in 1774, he entered into partnership with Matthew Boulton, a wealthy businessman and entrepreneur from Birmingham. By 1775, the first of many pumping engines had been produced. Watt continued to work on improving and developing steam engines and between 1781 and 1785, he patented sun-and-planet gearing, a double-acting cylinder, parallel motion linkage and the rotative engine. These developments were to transform industries such as textile manufacture. Watt might have had a hand in yet another major breakthrough in the industrial world had he only permitted the work to go ahead. Around 1784, he had considered a design for a steam locomotive, and an apprentice working with him, William Murdock, wanted to pursue the possibilities. However, Murdock was discouraged from taking the matter further and the opportunity was lost.

Watt was awarded an honorary degree by Glasgow University and was elected a fellow of the Royal Society in London in recognition of his work. Amongst his other achievements were the development of a pantograph, a process for letter copying, and an industrial cloth bleaching process. He retired in 1800 and died in Birmingham in 1819.

WILKIE, SIR DAVID
(1785–1841)
Painter

Son of a minister, born at Cults in Fife, Wilkie at the age of 14 was sent to study in the Trustees' Academy in Edinburgh. In 1804 he painted *Pitlessie Fair*, and the enthusiastic reception given to his *The Village Politicians* in 1806 prompted him to leave for London and its bigger market and lucrative commissions. *The Blind Fiddler* in 1807 confirmed his talent and its marketability, and a series of pictures showing the homely humour of domestic and humble life followed. What set them apart was a certain purity and transparency of style, clarity of observation, and skilful but unobtrusive technique. Wilkie was elected a Royal Academician in 1811. Around 1820 he changed his style, to a more 'old masterly' treatment, with grander themes, but his fame continued to rise. In 1830 he was appointed Painter in Ordinary to King William IV and was knighted in 1836. For his health he made a Mediterranean cruise in 1840, visiting Syria, Palestine and Egypt, but died on his way home and was buried at sea.